# The
# cAse
## for a
# cReatoR

## Resources by Lee Strobel

*The Case for a Creator*
*The Case for a Creator* Audio Pages®
*The Case for a Creator—Student Edition* (with Jane Vogel)
*The Case for Christ*
*The Case for Christ* Audio Pages®
*The Case for Christ—Student Edition* (with Jane Vogel)
*The Case for Easter*
*The Case for Faith*
*The Case for Faith* Audio Pages®
*The Case for Faith—Student Edition* (with Jane Vogel)
*Experiencing the Passion of Jesus* (with Garry Poole)
*God's Outrageous Claims*
*Inside the Mind of Unchurched Harry and Mary*
*Surviving a Spiritual Mismatch in Marriage*
    (with Leslie Strobel)
*Surviving a Spiritual Mismatch in Marriage* Audio Pages®
*What Jesus Would Say*

student edition

# The CASE for a CREATOR

A Journalist Investigates Scientific
Evidence That Points Toward God

# LEE STROBEL
with Jane Vogel

ZONDERVAN™

GRAND RAPIDS, MICHIGAN 49530 USA

**ZONDERVAN**™

*The Case for a Creator—Student Edition*
Copyright © 2004 by Lee Strobel

Requests for information should be addressed to:
Zondervan, *Grand Rapids, Michigan 49530*

---

**Library of Congress Cataloging-in-Publication Data**

Strobel, Lee, 1952–
    The case for a creator: a journalist investigates scientific evidence that points
toward God / Lee Strobel with Jane Vogel.—Student ed.
        p. cm.
    ISBN-10: 0-310-24977-5
    ISBN-13: 978-0-310-24977-1
    1. God—Proof, Cosmological.    2. Religion and science.    I. Vogel, Jane.
II. Title.
BT103.S772  2004
212'.1—dc22

                                                                                2004010002

---

*Interior design by Todd Sprague and Michelle Espinoza*

*Printed in the United States of America*

---

05  06  07  08  09  10  •  14  13  12  11  10  9 8 7 6 5

# Contents

# Acknowledgments

Special thanks to these student readers for reviewing the manuscript and offering comments:

Alex Bommelje
Amie Bommelje
Brian Masselink
Dana Masselink
Tina Oh
Janelle Schuurman
Dan Visser
George Visser
Rich Visser
Marie Vogel
Ross Wielard

## CHAPTER 1

# Science vs. God?

Can you understand science and still believe in God? I remember clearly when I first started asking that question—and how I answered it.

I was a fourteen-year-old freshman at Prospect High School in northwest suburban Chicago, sitting in a third-floor science classroom overlooking the asphalt parking lot, second row from the window, third seat from the front.

I already liked this introductory biology class. It fit well with my logical way of looking at the world. I was incurably curious—always after answers and constantly trying to figure out how things worked.

That's why I liked science. Here the teacher actually encouraged me to cut open a frog so I could find out how it functioned. Science gave me an excuse to ask all the "why" questions I was wondering about, to try genetic experiments by breeding fruit flies and to peer inside plants to learn about how they reproduced. To me, science represented the hard facts and the experimentally proven. I tended to dismiss everything else as being mere opinion, superstition—and mindless faith.

It was no accident that my admiration for scientific thinking was developing at the same time that my confidence in God was disappearing. While many of my classmates in Sunday school and confirmation class seemed to automatically accept the teaching of the Bible, I needed reasons for trusting it. When nobody wanted to hear my questions, I began to suspect it was because nobody had any convincing answers. And if there wasn't any scientific or rational evidence for believing in God, then I wasn't interested.

That's when, on that day in biology class, I began to learn about scientific discoveries that, for me, opened the door to atheism.

## HELLO EVOLUTION, GOOD-BYE GOD

My teacher explained that life originated millions of years ago when chemicals randomly reacted with each other in a warm ocean on prehistoric Earth. Then, through a process of survival of the fittest and natural selection, life-forms grew increasingly complex. Eventually, human beings emerged from the same family tree as apes.

Everything fell into place for me. My conclusion was that you didn't need a Creator if life can emerge unassisted from the primordial slime of the primitive Earth, and you don't need God to create human beings in his image if we are merely the product of the impersonal forces of natural selection. In short, I decided, you don't need the Bible if you have *The Origin of Species*.

By the time I was halfway through college, my atheistic attitudes were so entrenched that I was becoming more and more impatient with people of mindless faith. I felt smugly arrogant toward them. Let them remain slaves to their wishful

The Case for a Creator

thinking about a heavenly home and to the straitjacket morality of their imaginary God. As for me, I would follow the conclusions of the scientists.

## THE INVESTIGATION BEGINS

If I had stopped asking questions, that's where I would have remained. But with my background in journalism and law, demanding answers is part of who I am. So when my wife, Leslie, announced that she had decided to become a follower of Jesus, it was understandable that the first words I uttered would be a question.

I didn't ask it politely. Instead I spewed it out: *"What has gotten into you?"* I simply couldn't comprehend how such a rational person could buy into an irrational religious belief.

But in the months that followed, Leslie's character began to change. Her values underwent a transformation, and she became a more loving, caring, authentic person. I began asking the same question, only this time in a softer, more sincere tone of genuine wonderment: *"What has gotten into you?"* Something—or, as she would claim, Someone—was undeniably changing her for the better.

Clearly, I needed to investigate what was going on. And so I began asking more questions—a lot of them—about faith, God, and the Bible. I was determined to go wherever the answers would take me—even though, frankly, I wasn't quite prepared back then for where I would ultimately end up.

This multifaceted spiritual investigation lasted nearly two years. Because science had played such an important role in propelling me toward atheism, I spent a lot of time posing questions about what the latest research says about God. With an open mind, I began asking:

- Are science and faith incompatible? Am I right to think that a science-minded person must reject religious beliefs? Or is there a different way to view the relationship between the spiritual and the scientific?

- Does the latest scientific evidence tend to point toward or away from the existence of God?
- Are the teachings about evolution that spurred me to atheism all those years ago still valid in light of the most recent discoveries in science?

"Science," said two-time Nobel Prize winner Linus Pauling, "is the search for the truth."[1] And that's what I decided to embark upon—a search for the truth. I hope you'll join me as I retrace that journey. At the end you can decide for yourself which answers and explanations stand up under investigation.

## CHAPTER 2

# Beginning with a Bang: The Evidence of Cosmology

y eyes scanned the magazines at the newsstand near my home. A beautiful woman graced *Glamour*. Sleek, high-performance cars streaked across the front of *Motor Trend*. And there on the cover of *Discover* magazine, sitting by itself, floating on a pure white background, was a simple red sphere. It was smaller than a tennis ball, tinier than a golf ball—just three-quarters of an inch in diameter, not too much bigger than a marble.

As staggering as it seemed, it represented what scientists believed to be the actual size of the entire universe when it was just an infinitesimal fraction of one second old. The headline cried out: *Where Did Everything Come From?*[1]

Thousands of years ago, the Hebrews believed they had the answer: "In the beginning God created the heavens and the earth," says the Bible.

Everything began, they claimed, with the voice of God commanding light into existence. But is that a simplistic superstition or a divinely inspired insight? What do the cosmologists—scientists who devote their lives to studying the origin of the universe—have to say about the issue?

## For Quick Reference

cosmology = the study of the universe and how it began
cosmologists = scientists who study the universe and how it began

It seemed to me that the beginning of everything was a good place to start my investigation into whether science points toward or away from a Creator. I wasn't particularly interested in debates over whether the world is young or old. The "when" wasn't as important to me as the "how"—how do scientific models and theories explain the origin of everything?

## IN THE BEGINNING

"In the beginning there was an explosion," explained Nobel Prize–winning physicist Steven Weinberg in his book *The First Three Minutes*, "which occurred simultaneously everywhere, filling all space from the beginning with every particle of matter rushing apart from every other particle."[2]

The matter rushing apart, he said, consisted of elementary particles—neutrinos and the other subatomic particles that make up our world. Among those particles were photons, which make up light. "The universe," he said, "was filled with light."[3] (Interesting—that's what the Bible says too.)

But what caused that explosion? Did it just happen—first there was nothing, then there was something? Or did something—or Someone—make it happen?

Obviously, it's pretty difficult to get scientific data about something that happened before scientists were around to

The Case for a Creator

record the event. Still, scientists can draw reasonable inferences based on the evidence that they do have. And I wanted the very best analysis available—based on the hard facts of mathematics, the cold data of cosmology, and the most logical conclusions that can be drawn from them.

## THEORY 1: SPONTANEOUS EXISTENCE

Maybe you've heard the expression "Nature abhors a vacuum." I learned something even more interesting about vacuums as I explored the issue of the beginning of the universe. According to an article in the *Discover* magazine that caught my eye on the newsstand, "Quantum theory . . . holds that a vacuum . . . is subject to quantum uncertainties. This means that things can materialize out of the vacuum, although they tend to vanish back into it quickly. . . . Theoretically, anything—a dog, a house, a planet—can pop into existence."[4]

Wow! That's not a theory I've ever seen validated in real life. The article went on to say that "probability . . . dictates that pairs of subatomic particles . . . are by far the most likely creations and that they will last extremely briefly. . . . The spontaneous, persistent creation of something even as large as a molecule is profoundly unlikely." But still, this opens the possibility of "spontaneous existence"—which basically means, "Nothing caused it; it just happened."

However, is it really rational to believe that the entire universe simply exploded into existence by itself? Apparently, some people think so. For example, atheist Quentin Smith insists that "the most reasonable belief is that we came from nothing, by nothing, and for nothing."[5]

As for me, I wanted to know whether that belief stands up to scrutiny—or whether the laws of logic and the evidence of science point toward another conclusion: that something caused the universe to come into existence.

# THEORY 2: THE UNIVERSE HAS A CAUSE

The theory that intrigued me the most goes by the unusual name of the "*kalam* [pronounced KAH-lahm] cosmological argument." *Kalam* is an Arabic word that means "speech" or "doctrine," and the term actually comes out of Islamic theology. The argument has three steps.

## A Term to Know: Kalam Argument

1. Everything that begins to exist has a cause.
2. The universe began to exist.
3. Therefore, the universe has a cause.

## Step 1: Whatever Begins to Exist Has a Cause

In most people's experience, things don't just pop into existence, uncaused, out of nothing. You don't worry that, while you're away at school, a horse might pop into being, uncaused, out of nothing, in your room, and be there munching on your pillow when you get home. (Although think of the excuse that would be: "Teacher, the spontaneously existing horse ate my homework!") The evidence of experience suggests that whatever begins to exist *does* have a cause.

Still, my research had yielded at least one objection to *kalam*'s first statement. It comes from the wacky world of quantum physics, where all kinds of strange, unexpected things happen at the subatomic level—a level, by the way, at which the entire universe existed in its very earliest stages. It's the theory I mentioned earlier that things *can* materialize out of a vacuum.

I was only on step 1 of the *kalam* argument, and already I was stuck. I seemed to have two contradictory sets of evidence: my own experience (that things don't pop into existence without a cause) and the evidence of quantum physics (that something can materialize spontaneously out of a vacuum). I needed professional help.

I found it in a research professor named William Lane Craig. He has studied these issues for decades.

"Which statement is true," I demanded, "that objects don't pop into existence out of nothing, or that something *can* materialize out of a vacuum?"

"Okay, that's a good question," he said. "These subatomic particles the article talks about are called 'virtual particles.' They are theoretical entities, and it's not even clear that they actually exist as opposed to being merely theoretical constructs.

"However, there's a much more important point to be made about this. You see, these particles, if they are real, do not come out of nothing. The quantum vacuum is not what most people envision when they think of a vacuum—that is, absolutely nothing.

"On the contrary, it's a sea of fluctuating energy, an arena of violent activity that has a rich physical structure and can be described by physical laws. These particles are thought to originate by fluctuations of the energy in the vacuum.

"So this would not be an example of something coming into being out of nothing, or something coming into being without a cause. The quantum vacuum and the energy locked up in the vacuum are the cause of these particles."

That made sense—and it raised the interesting question of who or what would have created this quantum vacuum in the first place! Certainly its existence requires an explanation—and suddenly we're right back to the origins question. After all, this very active ocean of fluctuating energy would seem to have needed a Creator!

I had to admit that the universal experience of humankind seems to be that nothing simply pops into existence on its own, out of nothing. My conclusion was that step 1 of the *kalam* argument appeared to hold up.

## Step 2: The Universe Had a Beginning

One hundred years ago, the idea that the universe began to exist at a specific point in the past would have been very controversial. The assumption ever since the ancient Greeks has been that the material world is eternal. Christians have denied this on the basis of what the Bible teaches, but secular science always assumed that the universe always existed. So the discovery in the twentieth century that the universe is not an unchanging, eternal entity was a complete shock to secular minds. It was utterly unanticipated.

But I needed facts. How do we really *know* that the universe started at some point in the past? I discovered that scholars find evidence in two different ways: mathematically and scientifically.

***Mathematical reasoning:*** Early Christian and Muslim scholars used mathematical reasoning to demonstrate that it was impossible to have an infinite past. Because an infinite past would involve an actually infinite number of events, their conclusion was that the universe's age must be finite—that is, it must have had a beginning.

I have always been a reluctant student of mathematics (ask my algebra teacher if you don't believe me!), so this explanation was not particularly helpful to me. I needed an illustration.

Craig gave me one involving marbles. Imagine I had an infinite number of marbles in my possession, and that I wanted to give you some. In fact, suppose I wanted to give you an infinite number of marbles. One way I could do that would be to give you the entire pile of marbles. In that case I would have zero marbles left for myself. Infinity minus infinity = 0.

Another way to do it would be to give you all of the odd-numbered marbles. Then I would still have an infinity left over for myself, and you would have an infinity too. Infinity minus infinity = infinity.

Or I could give you all of the marbles numbered four and higher. That way, you would have an infinity of marbles, but I would have only three marbles left. Infinity minus infinity = 3.

Do you see how the idea of an actual infinite number of things leads to contradictory results? In the first case, infinity minus infinity is zero; in the second case, infinity minus infinity is infinity; and in the third case, infinity minus infinity is three. In each case, we've subtracted the identical number from the identical number, but we have come up with non-identical results.

That's because the idea of an actual infinity exists only in our minds. Working within certain rules, mathematicians can deal with infinite quantities and infinite numbers in the conceptual realm. However—and here's the point—it's not descriptive of what can happen in the real world.

The point of the illustration is that you couldn't have an infinite number of events in the past. Substitute "past events" for "marbles," and you can see the absurdities that would result. So the universe can't have an infinite number of events in its past; it must have had a beginning.

## An Infinite God?

If the idea of the universe being infinitely old leads to absurd conclusions, then what about the idea of God being infinitely old? Does mathematical reasoning also automatically rule out the idea of an eternal God?

Researcher William Lane Craig says no. "It rules out the concept of a God who has endured through an infinite past *time*. But time and space are creations of God that began at the Big Bang. If you go back beyond the beginning of time itself, there is simply eternity. By that, I mean eternity in the sense of time*less*ness. God, the eternal, is timeless in his being. God did not endure through an infinite amount of time up to the moment of creation; God transcends time."

***Scientific evidence:*** I also looked at scientific evidence that the universe had a beginning. Almost all scientists today believe that the universe began with the Big Bang (see timeline: "Looking for the Big Bang"), *not* that the universe has always existed. And predictions about the Big Bang have been consistently verified by scientific data. Unquestionably, the Big Bang model has impressive scientific credentials.

Scientific data seemed to support the first two premises of the *kalam* argument: that everything that begins to exist has a cause of its existence and that the universe began to exist. All that remained was the conclusion of the argument—and the absolutely staggering implications that logically flow from it.

## Step 3: Therefore, the Universe Has a Cause

Atheist Kai Nielsen said, "Suppose you suddenly hear a loud bang ... and you ask me, 'What made that bang?' and I reply, 'Nothing, it just happened.' You would not accept that."[6]

### Looking for the Big Bang

> **1915**
> Albert Einstein develops his general theory of relativity and is shocked to discover that, according to his equations, the universe should either be exploding or imploding. He adjusts his equations by putting in a factor that shows the universe remaining steady.

> **1920s**
> Russian mathematician Alexander Friedman and Belgian astronomer George Lemaître develop models that predict the universe is expanding. That means if you were to go backward in time, the universe would have had a single origin before which it didn't exist. Astronomer Sir Fred Hoyle mockingly calls this the Big Bang—and the name sticks.

The Case for a Creator

# The Big Bang: Good News or Bad News for Christians?

Maybe you've heard Christians denying the evidence for the Big Bang theory because they believe it contradicts the Bible's revelation that God created the world. But well-meaning, Bible-believing Christians have differing views on this issue.

For example, William Lane Craig believes that the Big Bang is one of the most plausible arguments for God's existence.

Adds astrophysicist C. J. Isham: "Perhaps the best argument . . . that the Big Bang supports theism [belief in God] is the obvious unease with which it is greeted by some atheist physicists."[7]

Agnostic astronomer Robert Jastrow admitted that, although details may differ, "the essential element in the astronomical and biblical accounts of Genesis is the same; the chain of events leading to man commenced suddenly and sharply, at a definite moment in time, in a flash of light and energy."[8]

You may have seen the bumper sticker that reads, "The Big Bang Theory: God spoke, and BANG! it happened." It's a little simplistic, but maybe it's not so far off.

## 1929

American astronomer Edwin Hubble discovers that light coming to us from distant galaxies appears to be redder than it should be. He explains this "red shift" as being due to the fact that the galaxies are moving away from us and the universe is expanding.

## 1940s

George Gamow predicts that if the Big Bang really happened, the background temperature of the universe should be just a few degrees above absolute zero.

## 1965

Two scientists accidentally discover the universe's background radiation—and it's only about 3.7 degrees above absolute zero, as predicted by the Big Bang model.

He's right, of course. And if a cause is needed for a small bang like that, then, argue many scientists, a cause is needed for the Big Bang as well. For many, the logical conclusion is that science confirms what the Bible says: that a Creator brought the universe into being.

After looking at the scientific evidence, I agreed that a cause sparked the Big Bang. But that's not the same thing as saying that the cause was God. In particular, I challenged whether any evidence suggests that the Creator is personal, as Christians believe, or merely an impersonal force, as many New Age believers maintain.

## What about Inflation?

The theory of inflation says that in the very, very early history of the universe, the universe went through a period of super-rapid, or "inflationary," expansion, growing from the size of a subatomic particle to about the size of a grapefruit. Then it settled down to the relatively slower expansion we observe today.

Some question whether this theory erodes the argument for creation. But since this inflationary period supposedly happened a microsecond *after* the Big Bang occurred, it really doesn't affect the question of the *origin* of the universe.

## THE PERSONAL CREATOR

I challenged William Lane Craig with my question about a personal Creator. "Don't arguments like yours just establish that a cause existed, but not whether it was, or is, alive or conscious?"

He explained that there are two types of explanations—scientific and personal (see the box "For Quick Reference").

The Case for a Creator

For example, imagine you walked into the kitchen and saw the kettle boiling on the stove. You ask, "Why is the kettle boiling?" Your mom might say, "Well, because the kinetic energy of the flame is conducted by the metal bottom of the kettle to the water, causing the water molecules to vibrate faster and faster until they're thrown off in the form of steam." That would be a *scientific* explanation. It describes the natural laws that make the water boil.

Or she might say, "I put it on to make a cup of tea." That would be a *personal* explanation. It describes the situation in terms of your mom and her decision to make tea. Both explanations are legitimate, but they explain the event in different ways.

So far, so good. But how does this relate to cosmology?

From further discussions with William Lane Craig, I came to realize that there *can't* be a *scientific* explanation of the first state of the universe. Because it's the first state, it cannot be explained in terms of earlier initial conditions and natural laws leading up to it.

## If Everything Has a Cause, What Caused God?

Remember—this argument is not that *everything* has a cause, but that everything *that begins to exist* has a cause. If God is eternal, as Christians believe and the Bible claims, then he had no beginning and thus no cause.

So if there is an explanation of the first state of the universe, it *has* to be a *personal* explanation—that is, an agent who has the will to create it.

## ALIVE TODAY?

Of course, even if the cause of the universe was personal, that doesn't necessarily mean that the Creator is still living today. Perhaps the Creator put the universe into motion and then ceased to exist.

My conclusion, though, was that it's certainly *plausible* that this being would still exist. After all, he transcends the universe and is therefore above the laws of nature, which he created. So it seems unlikely that anything in the laws of nature could extinguish him. And science gives us some other clues. As you'll see in the remainder of this book, many scientists believe there's good reason to believe the Creator has been involved in his creation since the time the universe sprang into existence. For example, the high information content in the cell offers strong evidence for an act of intelligent design of the first life, which took place after the universe began.

Plus, Christians believe this Creator has not remained silent, but has revealed himself in the person, ministry, and resurrection of Jesus of Nazareth. If that's true, then he's still around and still working in history.

So *is* it true?

Science can't tell us either way, which is fine. We're certainly free to look around for other evidence that the Creator still exists. Let's see if history establishes that Jesus really claimed to be the unique Son of God and then proved it by rising from the dead. (To weigh those facts for yourself, check out my book *The Case for Christ*.)

Beyond that, let's see if the Creator still answers prayers, if he still changes lives, and so forth. That's the kind of evidence I saw in my wife's life when she became a Christian—

the kind of evidence that started me thinking about the possibility of a personal God in the first place.

But if I was going to consider the case for a Creator seriously, I had to reexamine the claims of evolution that had originally led me toward disbelief in God. Were the atheistic conclusions I reached as a student valid? I was ready to find out.

## For Further Evidence

Craig, William Lane. *Reasonable Faith*. Wheaton, Ill.: Crossway, rev. ed., 1994.

Geisler, Norman, and Frank Turek. *I Don't Have Enough Faith to Be an Atheist*. Wheaton, Ill.: Crossway, 2004.

## CHAPTER 3

# Exploring Evolution: A New Look at Old Ideas

uestion: What do these people have in common?

- Nobel nominee chemist Henry F. Schaefer
- James Tour of Rice University's Center for Nanoscale Science and Technology
- Fred Figworth, professor of cellular and molecular physiology at Yale Graduate School
- The director of the Center for Computational Quantum Chemistry
- A total of one hundred biologists, chemists, zoologists, physicists, anthropologists, molecular and cell biologists, bioengineers, organic chemists, geologists, astrophysicists, and other scientists with doctorates from such prestigious universities as Cambridge, Stanford, Cornell, Yale, Rutgers, Chicago, Princeton, Purdue, Duke, Michigan, Syracuse, Temple, and Cal-Berkeley

Answer: All of them are skeptical about evolution.[1]

As a high school and university student studying Darwinism, I never knew that there were respected scientists who had serious doubts about whether the theory of evolution was enough to explain the complexity and diversity of life. I had been under the impression that it was only know-nothing pastors who objected to evolution on the grounds that it contradicts the Bible's claims.

## IMAGES OF EVOLUTION

I tend to be a visual thinker. Images stick in my mind for long periods of time. When I think back to my days as a student, what I learned in the classroom and through my eager reading outside of class can be summed up in a series of pictures.

I decided to take another look at each of the pictures that especially influenced me. Scientists have made a lot of discoveries since I first encountered evolution in my ninth-grade classroom. Would contemporary scientific research contradict or affirm the conclusions I reached so many years ago?

### Image 1: The Miller Experiment

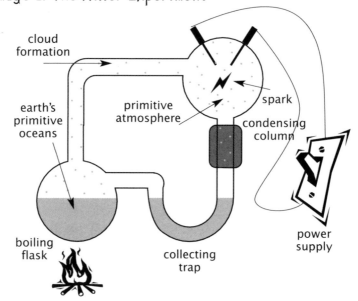

The Case for a Creator

# Definitions of Evolution

When people talk about evolution, they may mean different things.

Here are three common definitions of the word. In this chapter, we are referring to the third definition: Darwinism (or neo-Darwinism).

| Definition | Example | Do scientists agree on this? |
|---|---|---|
| Change over time | As nutrition and health care improved from the Middle Ages until now, the average human height increased. | Yes — there is agreement that there has been biological change over time. |
| Descent with modification | The child of one Asian and one Caucasian parent will have characteristics of both races. | Yes — there is agreement that this happens in the ordinary course of biological reproduction. |
| Darwinism: All living creatures are modified descendants of a common ancestor. Changes are the result of natural selection acting on random genetic mutations. | Humans and fruit flies are descended from the same early parent. | No — not everyone agrees that evidence points to a single ancestor or to purely random causes. |

The most powerful picture of all for me was the laboratory apparatus that Stanley Miller, then a graduate student at the University of Chicago, used in 1953 to reproduce the atmosphere of primitive Earth. By shooting electric sparks through it in order to simulate lightning, Miller managed to produce a red goo containing some of the amino acids that are the building blocks of life.

The clear implication—that life might have been created without the involvement of a Creator—had been largely responsible for convincing me there was no need for God.

Obviously, the significance of Miller's experiment hinges on whether he used an atmosphere that accurately simulated the environment of early Earth. At the time, Miller was relying heavily on the atmospheric theories of his doctoral adviser, Nobel laureate Harold Urey. But the consensus today is that the atmosphere of early Earth was not at all like the one Miller used (see the timeline "Early Atmosphere on Earth: Science's Changing Views").

## Early Atmosphere on Earth: Science's Changing Views

### 1953
For his experiment, Miller chooses a hydrogen-rich mixture of methane, ammonia, and water vapor, which is in keeping with what many scientists at the time consider accurate.

### 1966
*Proceedings of the National Academy of Sciences* asks, "What is the evidence for a primitive methane-ammonia atmosphere on earth? The answer is that there is *no* evidence for it, but much against it."[2]

The Case for a Creator

I discovered that if you attempt the experiment using what scientists now believe to be an accurate atmosphere, you don't get amino acids or anything else suggesting that life could develop from the mixture. Miller's experiment, once a great ally to my atheism, has been reduced to a mere scientific curiosity.

## Image 2: Darwin's Tree of Life

Darwin sketched his "tree of life" for *The Origin of Species* (see page 30) to illustrate his theory that all living things had a common ancestor. Starting with an ancient ancestor at the bottom, the tree blossoms upward into limbs, branches, and twigs that represent life evolving with increasing diversity and complexity.

It seems obvious to me that there's variation within different kinds of animals. I can see this illustrated in my own neighborhood, where we have lots of different varieties of dogs. Undeniably, there are variations *within* species of animals and plants, which explains why cows can be bred for improved milk production and why bacteria can adapt and develop immunity to antibiotics. This is called *micro-evolution*.

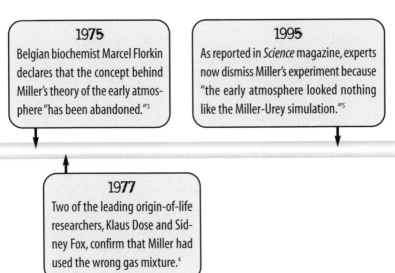

**1975**
Belgian biochemist Marcel Florkin declares that the concept behind Miller's theory of the early atmosphere "has been abandoned."[3]

**1995**
As reported in *Science* magazine, experts now dismiss Miller's experiment because "the early atmosphere looked nothing like the Miller-Urey simulation."[5]

**1977**
Two of the leading origin-of-life researchers, Klaus Dose and Sidney Fox, confirm that Miller had used the wrong gas mixture.[4]

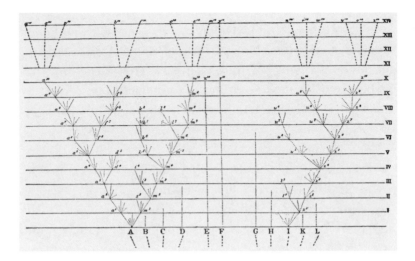

But I was intrigued by Darwin's claim that life began with simple, single-cell organisms that morphed over long periods of time—through *mutation* (accidental changes) and *natural selection* (changes that helped the species survive)—into every species, including human beings.

Based on observations of changes *within* species (for example, the fact that bacteria can develop into drug-resistant forms), Darwinists have theorized that evolution occurred *across* species. In other words, fish were ultimately transformed into amphibians, amphibians into reptiles, and reptiles into birds and mammals, with humans having the same ancestor as apes. Scientists call this theory *macro-evolution*.

## For Quick Reference

micro-evolution = gradual changes within a kind of animal (for example, over several generations of dogs)

macro-evolution = gradual change from one kind of animal to another (for example, from fish to amphibian to reptile)

Of course, descent from a common ancestor is true at some levels. Nobody denies that. For example, we can trace generations of fruit flies to a common ancestor. Within a single species, common ancestry has been observed directly. And it's possible that all the cats—tigers, lions, and so on—descended from a common ancestor. It's not a proven fact, say scientists, but it's conceivable.

So, is common ancestry true at higher levels? Darwin's theory predicted a long history of gradual change, with the differences slowly becoming bigger and bigger until you get the major differences we have now. But the fossil record, even in Darwin's day, showed the opposite. Instead of slowly developing, major groups of animals appear *suddenly* in the fossil record in what's called the "Cambrian explosion."

To get an idea of what happened in the Cambrian explosion, imagine yourself on one goal line of a football field. That line represents the first fossil, a microscopic, single-celled organism. Now start marching down the field. You pass the twenty-yard line, the forty-yard line, midfield, and continue steadily toward the other goal line. All you've seen this entire time are these microscopic, single-celled organisms.

You come to the sixteen-yard line on the far end of the field, and now you see the appearance of some sponges and maybe some jellyfish and worms. Then—*boom!*—in the space

## Darwinism Defined

When some people talk about *evolution*, they mean merely that there has been *change over time*. If that's all there was to Darwinism, then there wouldn't be any controversy, because everyone agrees there has been biological change over time.

Darwinism (updated as neo-Darwinism) claims much more than that—it's the theory that *all* living things are modified descendants of a *common ancestor* that lived long ago. According to Darwinism, every new species that has ever appeared can be explained by the result of natural selection acting on random genetic mutations.

of a single stride, at least twenty and as many as thirty-five of the world's forty phyla, the highest category in the animal kingdom, suddenly appear fully formed, without any of the ancestors required by Darwinism. To put this incredible speed into perspective, if you were to compress all of Earth's history into twenty-four hours, the Cambrian explosion would consume just one minute. Some experts believe that "*all* living phyla may have originated by the end of the explosion."[6]

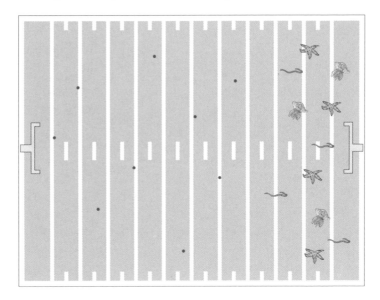

Now, nobody can call that a slowly branching tree! Some paleontologists, even though they may think Darwin's overall theory is correct, call it a lawn rather than a tree, because you have these separate blades of grass sprouting up. One paleontologist in China says the Cambrian explosion actually stands Darwin's tree on its head, because the major groups of animals—instead of coming last, at the top of the tree—come first, when animals make their first appearance.

Darwin's tree is a good illustration of an interesting theory, but it's not an accurate description of what the fossil record has produced. We don't have evidence that all animals share

The Case for a Creator

a common ancestor. Yet when I was a student, the next image helped convince me that we did.

## Image 3: Haeckel's Embryos

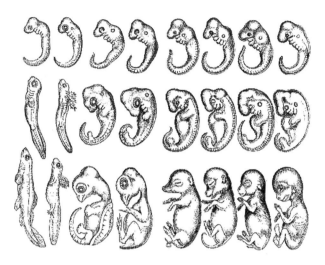

Ernst Haeckel was a nineteenth-century German biologist. His most famous drawings depict the embryos of a fish, salamander, tortoise, chicken, hog, calf, rabbit, and human side-by-side at three stages of development.

These images fascinated me when I first encountered them as a student. As I compared the embryos at their earliest stage, looking back and forth from one to the other, I could see they were extremely similar. I searched my mind, but I couldn't think of any logical explanation for this phenomenon other than a common ancestor. (For more on common ancestry, see the box "Berra's Blunder" on page 35.)

The real explanation, as it turns out, would have been far too bizarre for me to have even considered at the time.

## FAKING THE DRAWINGS

I got the real explanation from Jonathan Wells, a scientist who received his doctorate in molecular and cell biology from Cal-Berkeley, where he focused primarily on vertebrate embryology and evolution—the very things Haeckel was illustrating in his drawings.

"It wasn't until I was doing my graduate work that I began to compare actual photographs of embryos to what Haeckel had drawn," Wells told me. "I soon discovered that the similarities in the early stages were faked."

"Faked?" I repeated. "Are you sure?" It seemed inconceivable that the books I had relied on as a student could have so blatantly misled me.

"You can call them fudged, distorted, misleading, but the bottom line is that they were faked," he replied. "Apparently in some cases Haeckel actually used the same woodcut to print embryos from different classes, because he was so confident of his theory that he figured he didn't have to draw them separately. In other cases he doctored the drawings to make them look more similar than they really are. At any rate, his drawings misrepresent the embryos."

"That's amazing!" I said. "How long has this been known?"

"They were first exposed in the late 1860s, when his colleagues accused him of fraud."

I cocked my head. "Wait a minute—I saw these drawings in books that I studied when I was a student in the 1960s and 1970s—more than a hundred years later. How is that possible?"

"It's worse than that!" Wells declared. "They're *still* being used, even in upper-division textbooks on evolutionary biology. In fact, I analyzed and graded ten recent textbooks on how accurately they dealt with this topic. I had to give eight of them an F. Two others did only slight better; I gave them a D."

"If the drawings are so misleading," I asked, "then why did scientists continue to publish them for generation after generation of students?"

## Berra's Blunder

Have you seen drawings depicting the similar bone structures in a bat's wing, a porpoise's flipper, a horse's leg, and a human hand? I was taught that even though these limbs have been adapted for different uses, their underlying similarity is proof that they all share a common ancestor.

In 1990 a biologist named Tim Berra tried to illustrate this point by comparing the fossil record to a series of automobile models, saying that if you compare a 1953 and 1954 Corvette side by side, and then a 1954 and 1955 Corvette and so on, then it becomes obvious that there has been "descent with modification"—or a form of evolution. He said this is what paleontologists do with fossils.

Quite unintentionally, though, Berra had demonstrated that a series of similar forms does *not* necessarily point to natural evolution. After all, none of those Corvettes had evolved on their own through the natural effects of wind, rain, and rust; they had taken shape as a designer intentionally created and modified their structures.

The illustration is now referred to as "Berra's Blunder," because it opens the door for the possibility of an Intelligent Designer rather than undirected evolution.

"One explanation that's often given," he replied, "is that although the drawings are false, they teach a concept that's basically true."

With that, Wells picked up his book *Icons of Evolution* from the desk and flipped to the chapter on Haeckel. "Listen to this: One textbook shows Haeckel's drawings and says, 'Early developmental stages of animals whose adult forms appear radically different are often surprisingly similar.' A 1999 textbook has a slightly redrawn version of Haeckel's work and tells students, 'Notice that the early embryonic stages of these vertebrates bear a striking resemblance to each other.'[7]

"But this is *not* true. Biologists know that embryos are *not* most similar in their earliest stages."

Wells' explanation made me feel foolish for ever having believed the embryo drawings I had seen as a student. I felt a little like the victim of a con game, blaming myself for being so uncritical and naive in accepting what evolution textbooks and biology teachers had told me. I wondered what Wells would have to say about the fourth evolutionary image from my days as a student: the awe-inspiring fossil of a prehistoric creature that had once effectively silenced many of Darwin's critics.

## Image 4: Archaeopteryx, the Missing Link

This may be the most famous fossil in the world: the *archaeopteryx* (pronounced ar-key-OPT-er-icks), or "ancient wing," a creature that scientists date back 150 million years. With the wings, feathers, and wishbone of a bird, but with a lizard-like tail and claws on its wings, it was hailed as the missing link between reptiles and modern birds.

I sooned discovered, however, that scientists today consider the *archaeopteryx* to be a member of an extinct group of birds—not as part bird and part reptile.[8] After all, we see strange animals around today, like the duck-billed platypus, which nobody considers transitional but which has characteristics of different classes of animals. And even scientists who believe reptiles evolved into birds theorize that this occurred millions of years *after* the *archaeopteryx* appeared. So the

The Case for a Creator

"missing link" is still missing! In fact, the search to locate an actual reptilian ancestor for birds has resulted in some recent embarrassments for science. A few years ago the National Geographic Society announced that a fossil purchased at an Arizona mineral show turned out to be "the missing link" between terrestrial dinosaurs and birds that could actually fly. It had the tail of a dinosaur and the forelimbs of a bird. They called it the *Archaeoraptor*, and *National Geographic* magazine published an article in 1999 that said there was finally evidence that feathered dinosaurs were ancestors of the first bird.

The problem was that it was a fake. A Chinese paleontologist proved that someone had glued a dinosaur tail to a primitive bird!

Here's the question that has simply stumped scientists: How do you get from a reptile to a bird—which is an astonishingly huge leap, involving different breeding systems, bone structures, lungs, and distribution of weight and muscles—by some totally natural process? Evolution doesn't seem to have an answer, but the evidence does fit the intervention of a designer. (See the box "Berra's Blunder" on page 35 for a further exploration.)

## Image 5: From Ape to Human

Another picture—the parade of apelike creatures that morph into modern human beings—also summarizes what I believed in high school about the fossil evidence. From the cover of a 1998 edition of *The Origin of Species* to posters for the movie *Dumb and Dumberer*, this familiar image represents how I viewed the progress of human evolution.

When I was a kid, one of my favorite entries in the *World Book Encyclopedia* was "Prehistoric Man." I was fascinated by the part-ape, part-human called "Java man." The encyclopedia described how Dutch scientist Eugene Dubois, excavating on an Indonesian island in 1891 and 1892, "dug some bones from a riverbank." Java man, which he dated back half a million years, "represents a stage in the development of modern man from a smaller-brained ancestor."[9] He was, according to Dubois, *the* missing link between apes and humans.[10]

And I believed it all. However, I was blissfully ignorant of the full Java man story. "What is not so well known is that Java man consists of nothing more than a skullcap, a femur (thigh bone), three teeth, and a great deal of imagination," one author would later write.[11] In other words, the lifelike depiction of Java man, which had so gripped me when I was young, was little more than rank speculation.

When I was beginning to form my opinions about human evolution, I wasn't aware of what I have more recently discovered: that Dubois' shoddy excavation would have disqualified

## If Macro-evolution Is True

Evolutionary biologist and historian William Provine of Cornell University said that if macro-evolution is true, then there are five inescapable conclusions:

1. There's no evidence for God.
2. There's no life after death.
3. There's no absolute foundation for right and wrong.
4. There's no ultimate meaning for life.
5. People don't really have free will.[12]

Those are pretty radical concessions for an ardent Darwinist to make! What do you think? Are you convinced his five conclusions are true? Or do you have doubts about any of them?

## Did God Use Evolution?

Some scientists and theologians see no conflict between believing in the doctrines of Darwinism and the doctrines of Christianity.

For instance, biologist Jean Pond proudly describes herself as "a scientist, an evolutionist, a great admirer of Charles Darwin, and a Christian."

Personally, though, I couldn't understand how the Darwinism I was taught left any meaningful role for God. I was told that the evolutionary process was by definition *undirected*—and to me, that automatically ruled out a deity who was pulling the strings behind the scenes.

One recent textbook was very clear about this: "By coupling undirected, purposeless variation to the blind, uncaring process of natural selection, Darwinism made theological or spiritual explanations of life processes superfluous."[13]

the fossil from consideration by today's standards. Or that the femur apparently didn't really belong with the skullcap. Or that the skullcap, according to prominent Cambridge University anatomist Sir Arthur Keith, was distinctly human and reflected a brain capacity well within the range of humans living today.[14] Or that a 342-page scientific report from a fact-finding expedition of nineteen evolutionists demolished Dubois' claims and concluded that Java man played no part in human evolution.[15]

In short, Java man was not an ape-man as I had been led to believe, but he was "a true member of the human family."[16] This was a fact apparently lost on *Time* magazine, which as recently as 1994 treated Java man as a legitimate evolutionary ancestor.[17]

As I leaf back through my time-worn copies of the *World Book* from my childhood, I can now see how faulty science forced my former friend Java man into an evolutionary parade that's based much more on imagination than reality.

One anthropologist said that because of the lack of fossil evidence for prehistoric humans, trying to reconstruct the supposed relationship between ancestors and descendents is like trying to reconstruct the plot of *War and Peace* by using thirteen random pages from the book.[18]

Said Henry Gee, chief science writer for *Nature*: "The intervals of time that separate fossils are so huge that we cannot say anything definite about their possible connection through ancestry and descent." As a result, he said, the conventional picture of human evolution is "a completely human invention created after the fact, shaped to accord with human prejudices."

Then he added this clincher: "To take a line of fossils and claim that they represent a lineage is not a scientific hypothesis that can be tested, but an assertion that carries the same validity as a bedtime story—amusing, perhaps even instructive, but not scientific."[19]

## OUTDATED, DISTORTED, FAKE, FAILURE

After taking a new look at the pictures that had pointed me toward atheism when I was in high school, I could only shake my head.

I was left with an origin-of-life experiment that science has now rendered irrelevant, a tree of life that had been uprooted by the biological Big Bang of the Cambrian explosion, doctored embryo drawings that don't reflect reality, and a fossil record that stubbornly refuses to reveal the proliferation of missing links that Darwin himself predicted would be found. Doubts piled on doubts.

Are these images the only evidence for evolution? Of course not. But what happened to them is what happens time after time when macro-evolution is put under the microscope of scrutiny. No wonder the hundred scientists I mentioned at the beginning of the chapter made their doubts public. And that's not even taking into consideration the large number of other challenges to evolution that scientists have raised in recent years.

As for me, I finally came to the point where I realized that I just didn't have enough faith to maintain my belief in evolution as an explanation for the development and complexity of life. The evidence, in my opinion, was simply unable to support Darwin's grandest claims.

## THE CRY OF "DESIGN!"

I asked Jonathan Wells, the scientist who told me about the problems with Haeckel's embryo drawings, "If macro-evolution isn't a workable theory, then where do you believe the evidence of science is pointing?"

Speaking with conviction, Wells said: "I believe science is pointing strongly toward design. To me, as a scientist, the development of an embryo cries out, 'Design!' The Cambrian explosion—the sudden appearance of complex life, with no evidence of ancestors—is more consistent with design than evolution. Similarity across species, in my opinion, is more compatible with design. The origin of life certainly cries out for a Designer. None of these things make as much sense from an evolution perspective as they do from a design perspective."

"Let me get this straight," I said. "You're not merely saying that the evidence for evolution is weak and therefore there must be an Intelligent Designer. You're suggesting there is also affirmative evidence for a Designer."

## For Quick Reference

According to the Seattle-based Discovery Institute, the theory of Intelligent Design holds that certain features of the universe and of living things are best explained by an intelligent cause, not an undirected process such as natural selection.

"I am," he replied. "When you analyze all of the most current evidence from cosmology, physics, astronomy, biology, and so forth—well, I think you'll discover that the positive case for an Intelligent Designer becomes absolutely compelling."

I stood and shook Wells' hand. "That," I said, "is what I'm going to find out."

## For Further Evidence

Denton, Michael. *Evolution: A Theory in Crisis*. Chevy Chase, Md.: Adler & Adler, 1986.

Johnson, Phillip. *Darwin On Trial*. Downers Grove, Ill.: InterVarsity Press, 2nd ed., 1993.

Wells, Jonathan. *Icons of Evolution*. Washington, D.C.: Regnery, 2000.

## CHAPTER 4

# The Cosmos on a Razor's Edge: The Evidence of Physics and Astronomy

O n January 3, 2004, NASA's Mars exploration rover, *Spirit*, landed on the surface of Mars and sent a postcard—in the form of a post-landing signal—sixty-four million miles home. A few hours later, NASA websites had logged over one hundred million hits as fascinated earthlings logged on to view the stunning images sent back from the red planet. Less than two weeks later, President George W. Bush announced plans to extend human exploration in space, with a goal of extended manned missions to the moon as early as 2015, and then to Mars and "worlds beyond."

Imagine those first US astronauts landing on Mars. Picture them climbing out of the spaceship, stepping onto the desertlike surface of the planet— and finding an enclosed biosphere, a self-contained ecosystem. At the control panel of this Martian biosphere, the astronauts find that all the dials for its environment are set just right for life. The oxygen ratio is perfect; the temperature is seventy degrees; the humidity is 50 percent; there's a system for replenishing the air; there are systems for producing food, generating energy, and disposing of wastes.

The astronauts—and the hundreds of thousands of computer users downloading the images onto their monitors—would be amazed. Everyone from newscasters to politicians would be speculating: What country beat the US to a manned mission to Mars? Is it Sputnik all over again—did the Russians win the race this time too?

After all, the obvious implication of the biosphere is that some intelligent being had intentionally and carefully designed and prepared its environment to support living creatures. Certainly it couldn't be there by accident. Volcanoes didn't erupt and spew out the right compounds that just happened to assemble themselves into the biosphere. Its dial settings didn't happen to calibrate themselves to the exact right position so that life could exist inside.

And that, according to some physicists, is a powerful and persuasive analogy for our universe.

## THE FINE-TUNED HABITAT

Robin Collins, who has degrees in physics, mathematics, and philosophy, says, "Over the past thirty years or so, scientists have discovered that just about everything about the basic structure of the universe is balanced on a razor's edge for life to exist. The coincidences are far too fantastic to attribute this to mere chance or to claim that it needs no explanation. The dials are set too precisely to have been a random accident."

Collins is not alone in his conclusion that the fine-tuning of the universe is too significant to be a coincidence. (See the box "Coincidence? They Don't Think So" on pages 46–47). Many scientists have been impressed by something called the *anthropic principle.* The term, which comes from the Greek word *anthropos* for "man," basically means that the universe has everything we need to live—in other words, that the universe is "fine-tuned" for human existence.

## For Quick Reference

The **anthropic principle** is the observation that the universe has all the necessary and narrowly defined characteristics to make human life possible.

While studying the fine-tuning issue, I decided I not only wanted to explore the scientific evidence for the universe's precarious balancing act, but I also wanted to see if the anthropic principle could survive the challenge of skeptics. Collins once said that the facts concerning the universe's remarkable "just-so" conditions are widely regarded as "by far the most persuasive current argument for the existence of God,"[1] so I decided to talk with him in person about my questions.

## GRAVITY: DON'T TOUCH THAT DIAL!

Physics can get very complicated very quickly. Sometimes it helps to think in terms of examples that we can easily picture.

For instance, imagine a ruler, or one of those old-fashioned radio dials, that stretches all the way across the visible universe. It would be broken down into one-inch increments— billions upon billions upon billions of them. Collins said that the range of possible settings for the force of gravity can plausibly be taken to be at least this large.[2]

# Coincidence? They Don't Think So

Here's what some scientists are saying about the structure of the universe:

- "It is quite easy to understand why so many scientists have changed their minds in the past thirty years, agreeing that the universe cannot reasonably be explained as a cosmic accident. Evidence for an intelligent designer becomes more compelling the more we understand about our carefully crafted habitat."[3]

  —Walter Bradley, coauthor of *The Mystery of Life's Origin*

- "It is hard to resist the impression that the present structure of the universe, apparently so sensitive to minor alterations in numbers, has been rather carefully thought out.... The seemingly miraculous concurrence of these numerical values must remain the most compelling evidence for cosmic design."[4]

  —Paul Davies, former professor of theoretical physics at Cambridge University

- "The fine tuning of the universe provides *prima facie* evidence of deistic design."[5]

  —Edward Harrison, cosmologist

- "A common sense interpretation of the facts suggests that a superintellect has monkeyed with physics, as well as with chemistry and biology, and that there are no blind forces worth speaking about in nature."[6]

  —The late Sir Fred Hoyle, one of the world's most prominent astronomers

- "Through my scientific work I have come to believe more and more strongly that the physical universe is

*The Case for a Creator*

put together with an ingenuity so astonishing that I cannot accept it merely as a brute fact. . . . I cannot believe that our existence in this universe is a mere quirk of fate, an accident of history, an incidental blip in the great cosmic drama."[7]

—Paul Davies, physicist

• "A common sense and satisfying interpretation of our world suggests the designing hand of a super-intelligence."[8]

—Owen Gingerich, Harvard astronomy professor and senior astronomer at the Smithsonian Astrophysical Observatory

Right now, the force of gravity is set precisely at a certain point along this incredibly long continuum. As a result, life on Earth can flourish. But pretend the dial setting for the force of gravity were to be moved by just one single, solitary inch.

Immediately, the impact on life in the universe would be catastrophic! Animals anywhere near the size of human beings would be instantly crushed. Even insects would need thick legs to support themselves, and animals much larger couldn't survive. And that's just from moving the dial setting a mere inch compared to the width of the entire universe!

"As you can see," said Collins, "gravity has an incomprehensibly narrow range for life to exist. Of all the possible settings on the dial, from one side of the universe to the other, it happens to be situated in the exact right fraction of an inch to make our universe capable of sustaining life."

## THROWING DARTS AT AN ATOM

Gravity is just one factor that scientists have studied. One expert said there are more than thirty separate factors that require precise calibration in order for life to be possible in the universe.[9]

Collins named several other examples that he has personally investigated and that he believes make a case for Intelligent Design.

## A Quick Reminder

The theory of Intelligent Design holds that certain features of the universe and of living things are best explained by an *intelligent cause*, not a random and undirected process.

For example, there's the "cosmological constant," which is the energy density of empty space. It's part of Einstein's equation for general relativity, and it could have had any of an enormous range of values, positive or negative.

If it were large and positive, then galaxies, stars, and planets never could have formed. If it were large and negative, then the newly born universe would have collapsed upon itself. But it's calibrated at exactly the right value in order for the universe to be life-friendly.

I asked Collins for an illustration to help me understand this precision. "Let's say you were way out in space and were going to throw a dart at random toward Earth," he said. "It would be like successfully hitting a bull's-eye that's one trillionth of a trillionth of an inch in diameter. That's less than the size of one solitary atom!"

*Breathtaking* was the word that came into my mind. *Staggering*. "No wonder scientists have been blown away by this," I said.

"I'll tell you what," Collins said, "in my opinion, if the cosmological constant were the only example of fine-tuning, and if there were no natural explanation for it, then it would be enough by itself to strongly establish design."

Consider, though, what would happen if you added together the calibration of gravity and the cosmological constant. Then the fine-tuning would be to a precision of one part in a hundred million trillion trillion trillion trillion trillion trillion trillion. That's the equivalent of hitting one atom in the entire known universe!

And Collins wasn't through. "There are other examples of fine-tuning," he said. "For instance, there's the difference in mass between neutrons and protons. Increase the mass of the neutron by about one part in seven hundred and nuclear fusion in stars would stop. There would be no energy source for life.

"And if the electromagnetic force were slightly stronger or weaker, life in the universe would be impossible. Or consider the strong nuclear force, which binds protons and neutrons together in the nuclei. Imaging decreasing it by a little over 50 percent, which is tiny—one part in ten thousand billion billion billion billion, compared to the total range of force strengths."

"What would happen if you tinkered with it by that amount?" I asked.

"Since like charges repel, the strong nuclear force would be too weak to prevent the repulsive force between the positively charged protons in the atomic nuclei from tearing apart all atoms except hydrogen," he said. "And regardless of what they may show on *Star Trek*, you can't have intelligent life forms built from hydrogen. It simply doesn't have enough stable complexity."

I knew Collins could go on and on, but he had made his point. The way I saw it, it's supremely improbable that the fine-tuning of the universe could have occurred at random, but it's not at all improbable if it was the work of an Intelligent Designer. So it's quite reasonable to choose the design theory over the chance theory.

We reason that way all the time. Were the defendant's fingerprints on the gun because of a chance formation of chemicals or because he touched the weapon? Jurors don't hesitate to conclude that he touched the gun if the odds against chance are so astronomical.

If the universe were put on trial for a charge of having been designed, I would have to vote "guilty." Statistically, this would be a far stronger case than even the DNA evidence that is used to establish guilt in many criminal trials today.

## THE MULTIVERSE THEORY

Despite Robin Collins' confidence, however, an objection against the fine-tuning argument has been raised by some scientists in recent years. They say that the so-called "many-universes" or "multiverse" hypothesis debunks the conclusion that the universe was crafted by a Designer.

For example, England's Astronomer Royal, Sir Martin Rees, has conceded that if the six numbers that underlie the fundamental physical properties of the universe were altered "even to the tiniest degree," then there would be "no stars, no complex elements, no life."[10] But he tries to explain away this phenomenon by using the illustration of a large clothing store.

"If there is a large stack of clothing, you're not surprised to find a suit that fits," he says. "If there are many universes, each governed by a different set of numbers, there will be one where there is a particular set of numbers suitable to life. We are in that one."[11]

In other words, if ours is the only universe in existence, then fine-tuning is powerful evidence that an intelligence has tinkered with the dials. But that conclusion evaporates if there are many or an infinite number of universes. With enough random dial spinning, the odds are that at least one—our own—would win the cosmic lottery and be a livable habitat.

## Extraterrestrials: Are They Out There?

Although aliens like Captain Spock and Jabba the Hutt seem destined to live forever on DVD, more and more scientific discoveries are showing how incredibly improbable the right conditions for life are in the universe. Many scientists are concluding that intelligent life is far rarer than once thought. In fact, it may very well be unique to Earth. "The data imply that Earth may be the only planet 'in the right place at the right time,'" said science educators Jimmy H. Davis and Harry L. Poe.[12] Here's why:

1. Earth's atmosphere filters out harmful ultraviolet radiation while working with the oceans to moderate the climate through the storing and redistributing of solar energy.

2. Earth has plate tectonics, which cycles fragments of the earth's crust down into the mantle, resulting ultimately in a kind of thermostat that keeps the greenhouse gases in balance and surface temperature under control.

3. Earth is just large enough so that its gravity retains the atmosphere and yet just small enough not to keep too many harmful gases.

4. Earth is located in a "safe zone" in the galaxy:

- Out of range of most exploding supernova and hazardous giant molecular clouds (often located in the spiral arms);
- Far from the nucleus of the galaxy, where there's a massive black hole and more supernovae exploding;
- Shielded by Jupiter from the impact of life-threatening comets, which are attracted to Jupiter rather than to Earth because of Jupiter's tremendous gravitational pull;
- Protected by other planets from getting bombarded by asteroids from the asteroid belt (they mostly hit Mars and Venus, which are at the edge of the asteroid belt);
- On the very inner edge of the Circumstellar Habitable Zone, the only place where you can have low enough carbon dioxide and high enough oxygen to sustain complex animal life.

5. Earth's nearly circular orbit keeps it in the safe zone and maintains Earth at a steady temperature.
6. Earth orbits a sun with the right mass, the right light, the right composition, the right distance, the right orbit, the right galaxy, and the right location to nurture living organisms on a circling planet.
7. Earth's moon is the right size and distance so that it:

- Stabilizes the tilt of Earth's axis;
- Increases tides, which help to keep large-scale ocean circulation going and flush out nutrients from the continents to the oceans, keeping them more nutrient-rich than they otherwise would be.

Many Christians would have no theological problem if extraterrestrial life were discovered. God certainly could have created other life-populated planets that the Bible doesn't reveal. But at this point, an alien nation is pure speculation. What is scientifically demonstrated is that planet Earth is exactly what human life needs to survive. Chance—or design? You make the call.

I was genuinely curious: Is the hypothesis of many universes a reasonable alternative for skeptics who resist the idea of God? Does the fine-tuning argument hold up only for scientists who are also Christians? (For a related question, see the box "FAQ" on page 54.)

## THE COSMIC HOCKEY PUCK

Robin Collins at once identified the "self-reproducing inflationary universe" model proposed by André Linde of Stanford University as not only the most popular but the most credible version of the multiverse theory.

Linde suggests that our universe exists in a superspace that is rapidly expanding. A small part of this superspace is blown up by a theoretical "inflaton field," sort of like soap bubbles forming in an infinite ocean full of dish detergent. Each bubble becomes a new universe. In what's known as "chaotic inflation theory," a huge number of such universes are randomly birthed, thanks to quantum fluctuations, along various points of superspace. Thus, each universe has a beginning and is finite in size, while the much larger superspace is infinite in size and endures forever.

"Granted, it's highly speculative," Collins said. "There are an awful lot of loose ends with it. But since it's by far the most popular theory today—and I believe it should be taken seriously—let's not critique it right now. Let's just make the assumption that it's true."

# FAQ

**Q.** Are most of the scientists in the Intelligent Design movement Christians? And if so, doesn't that undermine the legitimacy of their science? Maybe they're only looking for what they want to find.

**A.** Let's look at each part of that question:

- First, no, the Intelligent Design movement is not an exclusively Christian movement. For example, there are agnostic and Jewish scientists who hold to the theory of Intelligent Design. The leading cosmological argument for a Creator came from a Muslim scholar.
- But even if all the scientists in the Intelligent Design movement *were* Christian, that wouldn't invalidate the movement. Every scientist has a motive, but motives are irrelevant to assessing the validity of scientific theories, a case in court, or an argument in philosophy. You have to respond to the evidence or argument that's being offered, regardless of who offers it or why. Their arguments have to be weighed on their own merits.
- Besides, look at it this way: If a scientist becomes persuaded by the evidence that there is a Creator and thus becomes a follower of God, should he or she then be disqualified from doing science in that area? Of course not. Let the evidence speak for itself. Is design the best explanation or not?

"All right," I said, nodding. "That's fine."

"Now, here's the main point: Even if Linde's theory could account for the existence of many universes, this would not destroy the case for design. It would just kick the issue up another level. In fact, I believe it would point *toward* design."

That was an interesting twist! "Why do you believe that?" I asked.

"I'll use an everyday example," he said. "My wife and I have a bread-making machine. Actually, it's defunct now, but we used to use it. In order to make edible bread, we first needed this well-designed machine that had the right circuitry, the right heating element, the right timer, and so forth. Then we had to put in the right ingredients in the right proportions and in the right order—water, milk, flour, shortening, salt, sugar, yeast. The flour had to have the right amount of a protein substance called gluten, or else it would need to be added. Everything has to be just right to produce a loaf of bread—otherwise, you get what looks like a burnt hockey puck.

"Now, let's face it, a universe is far more complex than a loaf of bread. My point is that if a bread machine requires certain specific parameters in order to create bread, then there has to be a highly designed mechanism or process to produce functional universes. In other words, regardless of which multiple-universe theory you use, in every case you'd need a 'many-universes generator'—and it would require the right structure, the right mechanism, and the right ingredients to churn out new universes.[13]

"Otherwise," he said, stifling a chuckle, "you'd end up with a cosmic hockey puck!"

## THE MANY-UNIVERSE MACHINE

Collins outlined for me some of the components necessary to produce functional universes:

- A mechanism to supply the energy needed for the bubble universes. That would be the inflaton field that Linde has hypothesized.
- A mechanism to form the bubbles. This would be Einstein's equation of general relativity.

- A mechanism to convert the energy of the inflaton field to the normal mass/energy that we find in our universe.
- A mechanism to vary the constants of physics so that by random chance it would produce some universes, like ours, that have the right fine-tuning to sustain life.
- The right background laws in place: the principle of quantization, the Pauli-exclusion principle, a universally attractive force between all masses—such as gravity. If just one of these components was missing or different, it's highly improbable that any life-permitting universes could be produced.

"And keep in mind," he added, "you would need to make trillions upon trillions upon trillions upon trillions of universes in order to increase the odds that the cosmological constant would come out right at least once, since it's finely tuned to an incomprehensible degree."

"What's your conclusion then?" I asked.

"It's highly unlikely that such a universe-generating system would have all the right components and ingredients in place by random chance, just like random chance can't account for how a bread maker produces loaves of edible bread. So if a many-universe generating system exists, it would be best explained by design.

"Those who believe in a Creator have nothing to fear from the idea that there may be multiple universes. There would still need to be an Intelligent Designer to make the finely tuned universe-generating process work. To modify a phrase from philosopher Fred Dretske: These are inflationary times, and the cost of atheism has just gone up."

## THE SUPERMIND

I thought for a few moments about Collins' explanation. Certainly it made sense that generating universes would require the right mechanisms, the right ingredients, and the right precision—all marks of Intelligent Design. But I was still mentally wrestling with something else. To me—admittedly, not a physicist—the whole concept of multiple universes seemed absurd.

I wasn't alone in that opinion. "The multiverse idea rests on assumptions that would be laughed out of town if they came from a religious text," said Gregg Easterbrook, contributing editor of the respected *Atlantic Monthly* magazine. "The multiverse theory requires as much suspension of disbelief as any religion. Join the church that believes in the existence of invisible objects 50 billion galaxies wide!"[14]

When I mentioned my skepticism to Collins, he listened carefully. "There's a reason you feel that way," he said. "You see, everything else being equal, we tend to prefer hypotheses that are natural extensions of what we already know."

## FAQ

**Q.** How can you argue that the Intelligent Designer of an imperfect world is a perfect God? If a perfect God created the world, wouldn't it be a perfect world?

**A.** From a biblical point of view, there isn't an expectation that nature would be perfect. The Bible says there has been decay or deterioration because evil entered the world and disrupted the original design. We're not given all of the specifics on how this happened, but the biblical book of Romans affirms that the natural world is groaning for its redemption, because something has gone wrong with the original creation. Based on the biblical account, we would expect to see both evidence of design in nature as well as evidence of deterioration or decay—which we do.

I wasn't sure what he was driving at. "Could you give me an illustration of that?" I asked.

"Sure," he said. "Let's say you found some dinosaur bones. You would naturally consider them to be very strong evidence that dinosaurs lived in the past. Why? Because even though nobody has ever seen dinosaurs, we do have the experience of other animals leaving behind fossilized remains. So the dinosaur explanation is a natural extension of our common experience. It makes sense.

"However, let's say there was a dinosaur skeptic. He was trying to rationalize away the bones you found. Let's suppose he claimed he could explain the bones by proposing that a 'dinosaur bone–producing field' simply caused them to materialize out of thin air."

"That's ridiculous," I said.

"And that's exactly what you would tell the skeptic," Collins continued. "You'd say: 'Wait a second—there are no known laws of physics that would allow that field to conjure up bones out of nothing.' But the skeptic would be ready for you. He'd reply, 'Aha—we just haven't discovered these laws yet. We simply haven't detected these fields yet. Give us more time, Lee, and I'm sure we will.'

"My guess is that you would still believe that dinosaurs existed, because this would be a natural extension of what you already know," Collins concluded. "On the other hand, arguably the skeptic needs to invent a whole new set of physical laws that are *not* a natural extension of anything we know or have experienced. You wouldn't buy his story. No way."

"You're saying, then, that an Intelligent Designer *is* a natural extension of what we already know?"

"Yes, I am," he replied. "Think about it, Lee—we already know that intelligent minds produce finely tuned devices. Look at the space shuttle. Look at a television set. Look at an internal combustion engine. We see minds producing complex, precision machinery all the time.

"So the existence of a supermind—or God—as the explanation for the fine-tuning of the universe makes all the sense in the world. It would simply be a natural extension of what we already know that minds can do. And, what's more, unlike the hypothesis that there are many universes, we have independent evidence of God's existence, such as a personal experience of the Creator and the other sort of evidence you're talking about in your book."

With that, one last question came to mind. "As you dig deeper and deeper into physics," I said to Collins, "do you have a sense of wonder and awe at what you find?"

"I really do," he said, a grin breaking on his face. "Not just with the fine-tuning, but in lots of areas, like quantum mechanics and the ability of our minds to understand the world. The deeper we dig, we see that God is more subtle and more ingenious and more creative than we ever thought possible. And I think that's the way God created the universe for us—to be full of surprises."

## For Further Evidence

Glynn, Patrick. *God: The Evidence.* Rocklin, Calif.: Forum, 1997.
For frequently asked questions on the evidence of physics and astronomy, as well as updates and resources, see Robin Collins' website at www.messiah.edu/~rcollins/ft.htm.

# CHAPTER 5:

# Mousetraps and Molecular Machines: The Evidence of Biochemistry

do you remember the board game Mousetrap®? You start with a pile of crazy mechanical gadgets—a bathtub on top of a pole, a plastic man ready to be launched from a springboard, an assortment of ramps and chutes—and, with each roll of the dice, you put them together to build a crazy contraption and trigger a chain reaction to drop a basket on your opponent's plastic mouse.

Sure, you could make a simpler mousetrap, but it wouldn't be nearly as much fun as turning the crank that rotates the gears that push the lever that moves the shoe that kicks the bucket that sends the ball down the stairs and into the gutter that leads to the rod that releases a second ball that falls through the bathtub and onto the springboard that catapults the diver into the washtub that causes the cage to fall and—if you're lucky—capture a mouse!

When I was researching this chapter, I kept hearing about a scientist who is bringing mousetraps into the field of molecular biology—not the wacky mousetraps of the board game, but your basic, hardware store–variety mousetrap. The scientist's name is Michael Behe, a biochemist who has made the simple mousetrap a symbol of some of the most complex science known: the science of the living cell.

## DOWN TO THE BASICS

When I interviewed Behe in his office at Lehigh University in Pennsylvania, he showed me an ordinary, run-of-the-mill mousetrap. "You can see how the parts work together," he said, pointing to each component as he described it.

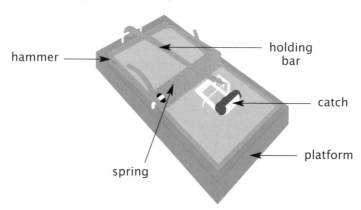

- There's a flat wooden platform to which all the other parts are attached.
- There's a metal hammer, which does the job of crushing the mouse.
- There's a spring with extended ends to press against the platform and the hammer when the trap is set.
- There's a catch that releases when a mouse applies a slight bit of pressure.
- And there's a metal bar that connects to the catch and holds the hammer back when the trap is set.

Behe explained, "If you take away any of these parts—the spring or the holding bar or whatever—then it's not like the mousetrap becomes half as efficient as it used to be. It doesn't catch half as many mice. Instead, it doesn't catch *any* mice. It's broken. It doesn't work at all."

The point Behe was making is that this basic mousetrap is as simple as it can get and still do the job. It doesn't have any extra parts you could take off and still achieve the same result. In scientific terms, when a machine can't be simplified any further, it is said to have *irreducible complexity*. In other words, you can't make it any less complex than it is and still have it work.

Why is this important? Behe says, "We've learned that the cell is actually run by irreducibly complex micromachines. [See the boxes "Factory in a Cell," "The Amazing Moving Cilium," and "The World's Most Efficient Motor."] The existence of these machines challenges a test that Darwin himself provided."

## For Quick Reference

A system is irreducibly complex if it has a number of different parts that all work together to accomplish the task of the system, and if you were to remove one of the parts, the system would no longer work.

The test Behe described was a little complicated, so he broke it into steps for me.

1. Darwin said in his *Origin of Species*, "If it could be demonstrated that any complex organ existed which could not possibly have been formed by numerous, successive, slight modifications, my theory would absolutely break down."[1]
2. Therefore, the complex molecular micromachines that make up cells must have been developed a bit at a time,

small step by small step. For instance, using the example of the mousetrap, maybe first there was just the platform, which evolved over time into a platform with a hammer, then a platform with a hammer and a spring, and so on.

3. But Darwin's theory of natural selection, or "survival of the fittest," says that the systems that work the best are the ones that survive and develop further. And a mousetrap that is just a flat wooden platform doesn't work. So according to natural selection, it wouldn't develop further; it would become extinct.

4. Like the mousetrap, molecular machines are irreducibly complex. Without all their parts in the right places, they don't work. Since natural selection chooses systems that are already working, any incomplete molecular machines would bite the evolutionary dust, not develop bit by bit. Oh, and one more thing: These micromachines are too complex for all of their parts to have come together all at once by random processes.

Behe motioned toward the mousetrap. "If the creation of a simple device like this requires Intelligent Design," he said,

## Factory in a Cell

"The entire cell can be viewed as a factory that contains an elaborate network of interlocking assembly lines, each of which is composed of a set of large protein machines. . . . Why do we call [them] *machines*? Precisely because, like machines invented by humans to deal efficiently with the macroscopic world, these protein assemblies contain highly coordinated moving parts."[2]

—Bruce Alberts, president of the
National Academy of Sciences

The Case for a Creator

"then we have to ask, 'What about the finely tuned machines of the cellular world?' If evolution can't adequately explain them, then scientists should be free to consider other alternatives."

## MESSING WITH THE MOUSETRAP

Behe's illustration of the mousetrap made some sense to me, but I know that it had generated quite a bit of controversy. One scientist argued that mousetraps can work well with fewer parts than Behe's mousetrap. I asked Behe, "Doesn't this mean that your mousetrap is *not* irreducibly complex?"

"No, not a bit," he said with a good-natured smile. "I *agree* there are mousetraps with fewer parts than mine. You can just prop open a box with a stick, or you can use a glue trap, or you can dig a hole for the mouse to fall into, or you can do any number of things.

"The point of irreducible complexity is not that one can't make some other system that could work in a different way with fewer parts. The point is that the trap *we're considering right now* needs all of its parts to function. The challenge of gradual evolution is to get to my trap by means of a series of many small changes. You can't do it. Besides, you're using your intelligence as you try. Remember, the claim of Darwinian evolution is that it can put together complex systems with no intelligence at all."

"Okay, but what about this?" I challenged. "Maybe an irreducibly complex system could develop gradually over time, because each of its parts could have another function that natural selection would preserve on the way toward developing a more complex machine."

I read the following excerpt from *Natural History*:

Take away two parts (the catch and the metal bar), and you may not have a mousetrap but you do have a three-part machine that makes a fully functional tie clip or

# The Amazing Moving Cilium

Cilia look like little hairs on the surface of cells. But under an electron microscope, scientists can see that cilia are, in fact, quite complicated molecular machines.

You have cilia lining your respiratory tract. Every cell has about two hundred of them, and they beat together—picture hundreds of microscopic synchronized swimmers—to sweep mucus toward your throat so you can cough it out. That's how your body expels little foreign particles that you accidentally inhale. But cilia have another function: If the cell is mobile, the cilia can row it through a fluid. Sperm cells would be an example; they're propelled forward by the rowing action of cilia.

What enables cilia to do this? A cilium is made up of about two hundred protein parts. Three kinds of parts—called rods, linkers, and motors—work together so the cilium can move. If it weren't for the linkers, everything would fall apart when the sliding motion began. If it weren't for the motor protein, it wouldn't move at all. If it weren't for the rods, there would be nothing to move. So, like the mousetrap, the cilium is irreducibly complex.

Darwinian evolution can't account for cilia. None of the individual parts can do the trick by themselves. You need them all in place. For evolution to account for that, you would have to imagine how this could develop gradually—but nobody has been able to do that.

Could the parts of the cilium come together by chance? Say there are ten thousand proteins in a cell. Now, imagine you live in a town of ten thousand people, and everyone goes to the county fair at the same time. Just for fun, everyone is wearing blindfolds and is not allowed to speak. There are two other people with your first name, and your job is to link hands with them. What are the odds that you could go grab two people at random with your name? Pretty slim. In fact, it gets worse. In the cell, the mutation rate is extremely low. In our analogy, that would mean you could only change partners at the county fair one time a year.

So you link with two other people—sorry, they're not the people with your name. Next year, you link with two other people. Sorry, wrong again. How long would it take you to link with the people who share your name? A very, very long time—and the same is true in the cell. It would take an enormous amount of time even to get three proteins together—and remember, the cilium is made up of two hundred protein parts!

paper clip. Take away the spring, and you have a two-part key chain. The catch of some mousetraps could be used as a fishhook, and the wooden base as a paperweight; useful applications of other parts include everything from toothpicks to nutcrackers and clipboard holders. The point, which science has long understood, is that bits and pieces of supposedly irreducibly complex machines may have different—but still useful—functions.[3]

Behe didn't flinch. "Of course it's true that some of the components of biochemical machines can have other functions. But the issue remains: Can you use a series of many small changes to get from those other functions to where we are?

"Could a component of a mousetrap function as a paperweight? Well, what do you need to be a paperweight? You need mass. You need to exist. An elephant, or my computer, or a stick can be a paperweight.

"The question for evolution is not whether you can take a mousetrap and use its parts for something else; it's whether you can start with something else—a paperweight—and make it into a mousetrap."

That's exactly what you do in the game Mousetrap®—take unrelated objects and make them into a mousetrap. But, of course, we do it by using our intelligence to figure it all out and put it together. And Behe reminded me of another problem: "Even if every part did serve some other function before it became part of the mousetrap, you'd still have the problem of how the mousetrap gets assembled."

"Explain further," I said.

"When people put together a mousetrap they have all the the parts in different drawers or something, and they grab one from each drawer and put it together. But in the cell, according to evolution, there's nobody there to do that. If you do any calculations about how likely this could occur by itself, you find it's very improbable. Even with small machines, you wouldn't expect them to self-assemble during the entire lifetime of the earth. That's a severe problem that evolutionists don't like to address."

## PUTTING THE MOUSETRAP IN THE TEST TUBE

Of course, the mousetrap is only intended to be an illustration to help people understand irreducibly complex cellular systems. There *is* a scientific way, however, to test Behe's concept of irreducible complexity.

Kenneth Miller, a biology professor who is also an outspoken evolutionist, suggested that one way to disprove Behe's theories would be to wipe out an existing multipart system and then see if evolution can come to the rescue with a system to replace it. If the system can be replaced purely by naturalistic evolutionary processes, then Behe's theory has been disproved.

Miller went on to describe an experiment by scientist Barry Hall of the University of Rochester to show how this apparently was done in the laboratory. Miller concluded: "No doubt about it—the evolution of biochemical systems, even complex multipart ones, is explicable in terms of evolution. Behe is wrong."[4]

I faced Behe squarely. "Tell me, has Hall proved through his experiment that your theory is incorrect?"

The Case for a Creator

Unflustered, Behe replied: "No, not really. Actually, Hall is very modest about what his experiment shows. He didn't knock out a complex system and then show how evolution can replace

## The World's Most Efficient Motor

I like fast cars. A friend recently gave me a ride in his exotic high-performance sports car and showed me what you can do when you generate enough revolutions per minute.

So I was fascinated to learn about a biological machine—the bacterial flagellum—that works like a rotary propeller and can spin 10,000 rpm.

Even the notoriously high-revving Honda S2000, with a state-of-the-art, four-cylinder, two-liter, dual-overhead-cam aluminum block engine, featuring four valves per cylinder and variable intake and exhaust valve timing, has a redline of only 9,000 rpm![5] This tiny flagellum (about 1/20,000 of an inch) has that record beat, and what's more, it can stop spinning within a quarter turn and instantly start spinning the other way at 10,000 rpm. No wonder Howard Berg of Harvard University called it the most efficient motor in the universe.

Drawings of the flagellum do look uncannily like a machine that human beings would construct. Sometimes when Michael Behe shows a drawing of the flagellum from a biochemistry textbook, people say it looks like something from NASA.

One scientist told me about his father, an accomplished engineer who was highly skeptical about claims of Intelligent Design. The dad could never understand why his son was so convinced that the world had been designed by an intelligent being. One day the scientist put a drawing of the bacterial flagellum in front of him. Fascinated, the engineer studied it silently for a while, then looked up and said to his son with a sense of wonder: "Oh, now I get what you've been saying." Simply seeing a depiction of the flagellum was enough to convince him it *must* have been the product of a designer.

it. Instead, he knocked out one component of a system that has five or six components. And replacing one component in a complex system is a lot easier than building one from scratch.

"For instance, suppose someone told you that natural processes could produce a working television set. You'd say, 'That's interesting. Why don't you show me?' He would then unplug a thousand television sets. Eventually, a strong wind would come along and blow one plug back into the outlet, and the TV would come on. He would say, 'See? I told you that natural processes could produce a working TV.' But that's not exactly what happened. He wasn't producing a new complex system; there was a glitch introduced and he showed that on occasion this can be fixed by random processes.

"That's a little like what went on with Hall's experiment with the bacterium *E. coli*. There was a complex system with a number of different parts, he knocked out one of them, and after a while he showed that random processes came up with a fix for that one part. That's a far cry from producing a brand-new system from scratch.

"But there's something equally important: Hall made it clear that he intervened to keep the system going while evolution was trying to come up with a replacement for the missing part. In other words, he added a chemical to the mixture that gave it the time to come up with the mutation that fixed the glitch. The result never would have actually happened in nature without his intelligent intervention in the experiment.

"Here's another analogy. Suppose you say you can make a three-legged stool by random processes. You take a three-legged stool and break off one leg. Then you hold up the stool so it won't fall over. Finally, a wind comes along, knocks down a tree branch, and it accidentally falls right where the missing leg had been. You're intervening to help the stool through the stage where it would otherwise have fallen over, and you've made it possible for the branch to fit in the right place.

The Case for a Creator

"Hall made it clear that he intervened so that he would get results that would never have actually happened in the natural world. And that is injecting intelligence into the system.

"When you analyze the entire experiment, the result is exactly what you would expect when you have irreducibly complex machines that depend on intelligent intervention. Unintentionally, he has shown the limits of Darwinism and the need for design."

## COMING TO CONCLUSIONS

In his work on the theory of irreducible complexity, Behe has come to two conclusions:

- First, he has taken Darwin at his own word and concluded that these biological machines could not have been created through a series of many small changes that Darwin's theory demands.
- Second, Behe has pointed out that there is an alternative that *does* sufficiently explain how complex biological machines could have been created.

"My conclusion can be summed up in a single word: *design*," Behe said as we came to the end of our interview. "I say that based on science. I believe that irreducibly complex systems are strong evidence of a purposeful, intentional design by an intelligent agent. No other theory succeeds; certainly not Darwinism."

My job—like yours—was to make my own conclusions from the evidence. I decided to look further into the science of cells and to explore where that evidence leads.

## For Further Evidence

Behe, Michael J. *Darwin's Black Box: The Biochemical Challenge to Evolution.* New York: Touchstone, 1996.

## CHAPTER 6

# DNA and the Origin of Life: The Evidence of Biological Information

instein said, 'God does not play dice.' He was right. God plays Scrabble."

At least, that's what analyst Philip Gold said. And when you consider the strings of letters that make up DNA, where the "language of life" is stored, it's quickly evident that Gold's quip makes sense.

With its familiar double-helix structure, DNA, or deoxyribonucleic acid, is basically the instruction manual for building the proteins that make up the cells of your body. We know that DNA stores that information in the form of a four-character code, made up of chemicals called adenine, guanine, cytosine, and thymine. Scientists represent them with the letters A, G, C, and T. Even with just four letters, the DNA alphabet spells out all of the information you need to build all the proteins necessary to keep you healthy.

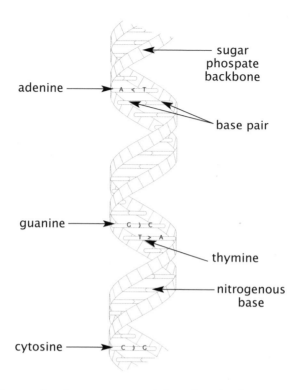

sugar phospate backbone

adenine

base pair

guanine

thymine

nitrogenous base

cytosine

When scientists announced that they had finally mapped the three billion codes of the human genome—a project that filled the equivalent of 75,490 pages of the *New York Times*—geneticist Francis S. Collins, head of the Human Genome Project, said DNA was "our own instruction book, previously known only to God."[1]

Are statements like that merely figures of speech? Or does the information in DNA really point to an Intelligent Designer who created the genetic material with its protein-building instructions? I decided to find out by talking with Stephen C. Meyer of the Discovery Institute, who earned his doctorate from Cambridge University and who is convinced that the information in DNA points toward an Intelligent Designer. His ideas and illustrations, many of which I drew on for this chapter, really helped me understand the issue of biological information.

# GENETIC SPELL-CHECK

We know from our experience that we can convey information with a twenty-six-letter alphabet—or even with just two characters, like the zeros and ones used in the binary code in computers. But it's important that the letters go in the right order. Order makes the difference between *unite* and *untie*.

The same is true for genes. In DNA, there are long lines of As, Cs, Gs, and Ts that are precisely arranged in order to assemble the amino acids into proteins. Different arrangements of characters yield different sequences of amino acids.

## For Quick Reference

DNA is the carrier of genetic information for all complex organisms.
A gene is a stretch of DNA that tells a cell how to make a specific protein.
Chromosomes are the strands of DNA on which the genes occur.
The total of all the genes in a living creature is called its genome.

For more than fifty years, as scientists have studied the six feet of DNA tightly coiled inside every one of our body's one hundred trillion cells, they have marveled at how it provides the genetic information necessary to create all of the different proteins out of which our bodies are built. In fact, each one of the thirty thousand genes that are embedded in our twenty-three pairs of chromosomes can yield as many as 20,500 different kinds of proteins.[2]

The presence of such specific information in DNA raises a critical issue. If you can't explain where the information comes from, you haven't explained life, because it's the information that makes the molecules into something that actually functions.

Bill Gates once said that DNA is like a software program, only much more complex than anything people have ever devised. At Microsoft, Gates uses intelligent programmers to

## Bill Gates and God

Is it legitimate to use an example of something from today—like Bill Gates developing software—to describe something from the beginning of life—like God creating DNA?

Actually, that way of reasoning is so much a part of scientific thinking that it even has a name: *uniformitarian logic.* In plain English, that means that what we know now about cause-and-effect should influence what we think caused something to happen in the past.

For example, said Stephen C. Meyer of the Discovery Institute, let's say you find a certain kind of ripple marks preserved from the ancient past in layers of rock. And let's say that in the present day you see the same sort of ripple marks forming in lake beds as the water evaporates. Based on what you know about the cause (evaporating water) and the effect (ripple marks) today, you can reasonably propose a similar cause for the same effect in the past.

So if we observe that complex information like computer programs develops without anyone writing it, we can reasonably presume that similarly complex information in the DNA of early cells developed on its own. If our experience shows, however, that information always has an intelligent source—which it clearly does—then logically we should expect that to be true of DNA.

produce software. In an analagous way, many scientists today believe that it makes sense that an intelligent being "programmed" DNA.

## THE MISSING SOUP

While the theory of an intelligent source for DNA and living cells makes sense to me, I wasn't about to ignore other theories about the origin of life.

In 1871, Charles Darwin wrote a letter in which he speculated that life might have originated when a protein compound was chemically formed "in some warm little pond" when all the right components came together. This concept is so widely accepted today that most theories about the origin of life presuppose this "prebiotic soup" of organic compounds as the environment in which life began.

I decided to explore the evidence for this primeval ocean. The trouble was, I couldn't find any evidence.

If this prebiotic soup had existed, I learned, it would have been rich in amino acids. Therefore, there would have been a lot of nitrogen, because amino acids are nitrogenous. So when scientists examine the earliest sediments of Earth, they should find large deposits of nitrogen-rich minerals.

But those deposits have never been located. (See the box "Got Soup?")

## Got Soup?

Looking for evidence of a prehistoric ocean of chemicals that has come to be called "prebiotic soup," these scientists came up hungry.

- "The nitrogen content of early organic matter is relatively low—just .015 percent. From this we can be reasonably certain that there never was any substantial amount of 'primitive soup' on Earth when pre-Cambrian sediments were formed; if such a soup ever existed it was only for a brief period of time."[3]

  —Jim Brooks, geochemist

- "Considering the way the prebiotic soup is referred to in so many discussions of the origin of life as an already established reality, it comes as something of a shock to realize that there is absolutely no positive evidence for its existence."[4]

  —Michael Denton, geneticist

This was an astounding discovery for me! After all, scientists routinely talk about the prebiotic soup as if it were a given. I got another surprise as I continued my investigation: I ran into my old friend, Stanley Miller—the scientist who tried to recreate early Earth's atmosphere and spark it with electricity. (See chapter 3.) Although his experiment used an atmosphere that scientists now recognize as unrealistic, he did manage to create two or three of the protein-forming amino acids out of the twenty-two that exist.

What I hadn't known, though, is that Miller's amino acids reacted very quickly with the other chemicals in the chamber, resulting in a brown sludge that's not life-friendly at all. The way scientists dealt with this in their experiments has been to remove these other chemicals in the hope that further reactions could take the experiment in a life-friendly direction.

So instead of simulating a natural process, they interfered in order to get the outcome they wanted. You might say, in fact, that they were acting as intelligent designers! This was not the direction I expected the Stanley Miller experiment to lead!

Undoubtedly, obstacles to the formation of life on primitive Earth would have been extremely challenging, even if the world were awash with an ocean of the right stuff. But there were other possibilities. In fact, I quickly learned from Stephen Meyer that there are three basic options.

## SCENARIO 1: RANDOM CHANCE

Although the idea of life forming by random chance isn't taken seriously right now among scientists, the idea is still very much alive at the popular level. Many college students, for example, speculate that if you let amino acids randomly interact over millions of years, life is somehow going to emerge.

The problems with that theory became apparent to me pretty quickly. Imagine trying to make even a simple book by throwing Scrabble letters onto the floor. Or imagine closing your eyes and picking Scrabble letters out of a bag. Are you going to produce *Hamlet* in anything like the time of the known universe? Even a simple protein molecule is so rich in information that the entire history of the universe since the Big Bang wouldn't give you the time you would need to generate that molecule by chance. (See the box "Books by Accident.")

Even if the first molecule had been much simpler than those today, there's a minimum structure that a protein has to have for it to function. Did you know that you don't get that structure in a protein unless you have at least seventy-five amino acids or so? Think about what you'd need for a protein molecule to form by chance:

- First, you need the right bonds between the amino acids.
- Second, amino acids come in right-handed and left-handed versions, and you have to get only left-handed ones.
- Third, the amino acids must link up in a specified sequence, like letters in a sentence.

Run the odds of these things falling into place on their own and you find that the probabilities of forming a rather short functional protein at random would be one chance in a hundred thousand trillion trillion trillion trillion trillion trillion trillion trillion trillion trillion. That's a ten with 125 zeroes after it!

And that would be only one protein molecule—a fairly simple cell would need between three hundred and five hundred protein molecules.

When you look at those odds, you can see why, since the 1960s, scientists have abandoned the idea that chance played any significant role in the origin of DNA or proteins. (See the box "Almost a Miracle.")

## SCENARIO 2: NATURAL SELECTION

Random chance might not account for the origin of life, but what about natural selection acting on chance variations?

The problem with this theory is that you can't have natural selection *before* you have life. The theory of natural selection requires reproduction to work. Organisms reproduce, their offspring have variations, the ones that are better adapted to their environment survive better, and so those adaptations are preserved and passed on to the next generation.

In order to have reproduction, there has to be cell division, with information-rich DNA and proteins. But that's the problem—those are the very things I was trying to explain!

As Meyer quipped, it's like the story about the guy who falls into a deep hole and realizes he needs a ladder to get out. So he climbs out, goes home, gets a ladder, jumps back into the hole, and climbs out. It begs the question.

## A Term You Might Encounter: "RNA-1st Hypothesis"

The RNA-1st hypothesis that says the first cell reproduced by using RNA instead of DNA. Like DNA, RNA can store information and even replicate. Some small viruses use RNA as their genetic material. But because RNA molecules are simpler than DNA, some scientists thought they might be more likely to form through natural processes or pure chance.

Although popular for a while, the RNA theory has generated more than its share of skeptics. The main problem is that the RNA molecule would need a certain minimal amount of information to function, just as DNA would—so we're right back to the same problem of where the information came from in the first place.

## SCENARIO 3: CHEMICAL ATTRACTION

By the early 1970s, most origin-of-life scientists were disappointed with the options of random chance and natural selection. As a result, some explored a third possibility: that proteins and DNA could put themselves together.

At first, that makes some sense. There are lots of cases in nature in which the chemical attractions of different elements will explain how the molecule formed. Salt crystals are a good example. Chemical forces of attraction cause sodium ions, Na+, to bond with chloride ions, Cl−, in order to form highly ordered patterns within a crystal of salt—NaCl. Scientists theorized that similar chemical attractions may have caused DNA's four-letter alphabet to link together.

But Meyer pointed out to me that there are huge difficulties with this theory. Remember, he said, that the genetic information in DNA is spelled out by the chemical letters A, C, G, and T. What if there were a force that made A automatically attract

### "Almost a Miracle"

Dr. Francis Crick, codiscoverer of the double-helix structure of DNA, has conceded: "An honest man, armed with all the knowledge available to us now, could only state that in some sense, the origin of life appears at the moment to be almost a miracle, so many are the conditions which would have had to have been satisfied to get it going."[6]

a G? You'd just have a repetitive sequence: AGAGA GAG—in much the same way that a salt crystal is a repetitive sequence of NaCl over and over. Would that give you a gene that could produce a protein?

Think of it this way: Open any book; you won't see the word *the* repeating over and over and over. If all you had were repeating characters in DNA, the assembly instructions would tell amino acids to assemble in the same way over and over again. You wouldn't be able to build all the many different kinds of protein molecules you need for a living cell to function. It would be like handing a person an instruction book for how to build an automobile, but all the book said was "the-the-the-the-the-the." You couldn't hope to convey all the necessary information with that one-word vocabulary.

To me, this absolutely doomed the idea of chemical attractions accounting for the information in DNA. But there is yet another problem with this theory.

If you study DNA, you find that certain bonds *are* caused by chemical attractions. For instance, there are bonds between the sugar and phosphate molecules that form the two twisting backbones of the DNA molecule.

However, there's one place where there are *no* chemical bonds, and that's between the chemical letters in DNA's assembly instructions. The letters that spell out the DNA message don't interact chemically with each other in any significant way. Also, they're totally interchangeable. As Meyer explained, each base can attach with equal facility at any site along the DNA backbone.

Picture a refrigerator with magnetic letters sticking to it to spell the word *INFORMATION.*

You know that there are magnetic attractions there; that's why the magnetic letters stick to the refrigerator. But there isn't any magnetic force *between* letters. You can pick one off the fridge and put it wherever you want to spell whatever you want.

Now, in DNA, each individual letter is chemically bonded to the sugar-phosphate backbone of the molecule. That's how they're attached to the DNA's structure. But—and here's the key point that Meyer stressed to me—*there is no attraction or bonding between the individual letters themselves.* So there's nothing chemically that forces them into any particular sequence. The sequencing has to come from somewhere else.

Suppose I showed you the magnetic letters sticking to the refrigerator and asked you, "How did this word *INFORMA-TION* get here?" What would you say?

The answer, of course, is intelligence that comes from outside the system. Neither chemistry nor physics arranged the letters this way. It was my choice. And in DNA, neither chemistry nor physics arranges the letters into the assembly instructions for proteins. The cause comes from outside the system.

It was starting to look strongly to me as if that cause might be an Intelligent Designer.

## THE INFORMATION AGE

Today, said Meyer, we buy information, we sell it, we send it down wires and bounce it off satellites—and we know it invariably comes from intelligent agents. So what do we make of the fact that there's information in life? What do we make of the fact that DNA stores far more information in a smaller space than the most advanced supercomputer on the planet?

Information is a characteristic of a mind. And the evidence of genetics and biology seems to point toward the existence of a mind that's far greater than our own—a conscious, purposeful, rational Intelligent Designer who's amazingly creative.

The argument was compelling: An intelligent entity has quite literally spelled out evidence of his existence through the four chemical letters in the genetic code. It's almost as if the Creator autographed every cell.

After months of investigating scientific evidence for God, the case for a Creator was accumulating at a remarkable pace, and I could sense I was approaching the conclusion of my quest. It was time to synthesize and digest what I had learned— and ultimately to come to a conclusion that would have vast and life-changing implications.

## For Further Evidence

Meyer, Stephen C. "The Explanatory Power of Design: DNA and the Origin of Information." In *Mere Creation*, ed. William A. Dembski. Downers Grove, Ill.: InterVarsity Press, 1998.

Newman, Robert C., ed. *What's Darwin Got to Do with It?* Downers Grove, Ill: InterVarsity Press, 2000.

*Unlocking the Mystery of Life* DVD. La Habra, Calif.: Illustra Media, 2002.

## CHAPTER 7

# Decision Time: Is There a Case for a Creator?

t was decision time. I was ready to weigh the evidence and draw my conclusions: Does the latest scientific evidence tend to point toward or away from the existence of God? In other words, do facts support faith?

Actually, there's a lot of misunderstanding about faith. Some people believe faith actually contradicts facts.

However, that's certainly not my understanding. I see faith as being a reasonable step in the same direction that the evidence is pointing. If the facts of science and history point toward God, then it seems rational and logical for me to respond to those facts by investing my trust in him.

The more I analyzed the scientific data, the more difficult it became for me to believe in the Darwinism that had undergirded my atheism for so many years. To be honest, it simply seemed too far-fetched to be credible. To embrace Darwinism and its underlying premise of naturalism, I realized that I would have to believe that:

- Nothing produces everything.
- Nonlife produces life.
- Randomness produces fine-tuning.
- Chaos produces information.
- Unconsciousness produces consciousness.
- Non-reason produces reason.

Based on this, I was forced to conclude that Darwinism would require a blind leap of faith that I was not willing to take. Simply put, the central pillars of evolutionary theory quickly rotted away when exposed to scrutiny.

Naturalism and Darwinism had no explanation for the creation of the universe; for the appearance of the first living cell; for the fossil record that shows the sudden appearance of fully formed, complex creatures in the Cambrian explosion; for the "irreducibly complex" biological systems that Michael Behe had described; or for the source of the information in DNA. No wonder Michael Denton, a research scientist in human molecular genetics, gave his devastating critique of Darwinism the title *Evolution: A Theory in Crisis.*

## THE CASE FOR A CREATOR

On the other hand, the evidence from the latest scientific research is convincing more and more scientists that facts support faith in a Creator as never before. "Only a rookie who knows nothing about science would say science takes away from faith," said nanoscientist James Tour of Rice University. "If you really study science, it will bring you closer to God."[1]

You can draw your own conclusions from reading this book. But for me, the evidence from cosmology, physics, biochemistry, and genetics compiled a convincing case that a Creator exists.

## Cosmology

Our universal experience dictates that whatever begins to exist has a cause. Science now affirms that the universe began to exist. (As Stephen Hawking said, "Almost everyone now believes that the universe, and time itself, had a beginning at the Big Bang.")[2] Therefore, the logical conclusion is that the universe had a cause.

## Physics

One of the most striking discoveries of modern science has been that the laws and constants of physics unexpectedly conspire in an extraordinary way to make the universe habitable for life. Physicist and philosopher Robin Collins showed that mere chance cannot reasonably account for this mind-boggling calibration of physics. A more logical explanation is a Creator.

## Biochemistry

Darwin himself said, "If it could be demonstrated that any complex organ existed which could not possibly have been formed by numerous, successive, slight modifications, my theory would absolutely break down." Biochemist Michael Behe has demonstrated exactly that through his description of "irreducibly complex" molecular machines. These incredible biological systems point toward a Designer. As Behe told me: "I believe that irreducibly complex systems are strong evidence of a purposeful, intentional design by an intelligent agent."

## Biological information

DNA contains a four-letter chemical alphabet that spells out precise assembly instructions for all the proteins from which our bodies are made. No theory has come close to explaining how this information got into biological matter by natural means. On the contrary, whenever we find this kind of information—for instance, in a book or computer code—we know it has an intelligent source. Finding it in DNA, then, indicates the existence of an Intelligent Designer.

The findings of science, though, can only take us so far. At some point, the facts demand a response. When we decide not merely to ponder the abstract concept of a Designer but to embrace him as our own—to make him our "true God"—then we can meet him personally, relate to him daily, and spend eternity with him as he promises.

And that, as a young medical doctor and his wife learned, changes everything.

## FROM SCIENCE TO GOD

No one was more surprised by the scientific evidence for God than the soft-spoken, silver-haired, seventy-seven-year-old physician who was sitting across from me in a booth at a Southern California restaurant.

His story is an example of the power of science to point seekers toward God. However, it's something else too—a road map for how you might want to proceed if you're personally interested in seeing whether faith in God is supported by the facts.

Viggo Olsen is a brilliant surgeon whose life was steeped in science. Graduating with honors from medical school, he later became a fellow of the American Board of Surgeons. In fact, his name has a whole raft of letters after it—M.S., M.D., Litt.D., D.H., F.A.C.S., F.I.C.S., and D.T.M.&H. He attributed his spiritual skepticism to his knowledge of the scientific world.

"I viewed Christianity and the Bible through agnostic eyes," he said. "My wife, Joan, was a skeptic too. We believed there was no independent proof that any Creator exists. Rather, we believed life came into being through evolutionary processes."

The problem was Joan's parents, both devout Christians. When Viggo and Joan visited them on their way to starting his first internship at a New York City hospital, they got an earful of what they considered religious propaganda. In late-night discussions, Viggo and Joan would patiently explain why Christianity was inconsistent with contemporary science. Finally, in frustration at two o'clock one morning around the kitchen table, they agreed to examine the evidence for themselves.

Viggo implied his search would be sincere and honest, but inwardly he had already hatched a plan. "My intent was not to do an objective study at all," he recalled. "Just like a surgeon incises a chest, we were going to slash into the Bible and dissect out all its embarrassing scientific mistakes."

Back home, Viggo and Joan labeled a piece of paper: "Scientific Mistakes in the Bible," figuring they could easily fill it. They worked out a system under which they would discuss with each other what they were learning in their investigation. At the end, there would always be more unanswered questions. While Viggo was working at the hospital, Joan would research the issues left hanging. Then they would switch roles, like a tag team, as they took turns digging into the evidence.

Problems quickly emerged—but not the kind they were anticipating. "We were having trouble finding those scientific mistakes," he said. "We'd find something that seemed to be an error, but on further reflection and study, we saw that our understanding had been shallow. That made us sit up and take notice."

Then a student passed along a book called *Modern Science and Christian Faith*. Each of its thirteen chapters was written by a different scientist about the evidence in his field that pointed toward God. Even though it was published before many of the eye-popping scientific discoveries that I've described in this book, the evidence was enough to stun Viggo and Joan.

"It blew our minds!" Viggo said. "For the first time we began to see there were reasons behind Christianity."

## THE ADVENTURE OF A LIFETIME

They devoured that book, plus many others that were listed in its bibliography. As they analyzed the evidence, they came to several conclusions.

First, they decided the universe was not eternal, but that it must have come into being at a certain point. Because the universe is packed with power—heat energy, atomic energy, and so forth—they reasoned that it must have been brought into being by some *mighty force.*

Second, they looked at the obvious design of the universe and the human body, all the way down to organs and cells, concluding that the power that brought the universe into existence must also be *intelligent.*

Third, they decided that, as great as the human intellect is, there is something even higher—the ability of people *to*

---

### The Identity of the Creator

Viggo and Joan Olsen discovered that the portrait of the Creator that emerges from the scientific data is uncannily consistent with the description of the God whose identity is spelled out in the pages of the Bible.

- *Creator?* "In the beginning you laid the foundation of the earth, and the heavens are the work of your hands."[3]
- *Enormously powerful?* "The LORD is . . . great in power."[4]
- *Intelligent and rational?* "How many are your works, O LORD! In wisdom you made them all; the earth is full of your creatures."[5]
- *Caring?* "The earth is full of his unfailing love."[6]

---

The Case for a Creator

*empathize, to love, and to have compassion.* Since the Creator must be greater than his creatures, he must also have those same qualities.

Based on evidence and reasoning independent of the Bible, they were able to answer the first of the three questions that formed the basis of their investigation: "Is there a God who created the universe?" They surprised themselves with their verdict: Yes, a personal Creator-God does exist. (See the box "The Identity of the Creator.")

With this established, they began exploring their next two broad questions: "Did God reveal himself to humankind through the Bible or other sacred scriptures? And is Jesus the Son of God—deity united with humanity—and can he help us as he claimed?"

The investigation continued into those topics. One day, while Viggo was working at the hospital, he formulated what he thought was a powerful argument against Christianity. "I was really proud of it," he told me, reliving the scene as if it were last month. "I spent all day mentally honing it. I couldn't wait to tell Joan!"

At the end of his shift, he walked the three blocks to their small apartment. Standing in the entryway, he told Joan his new objection to Christianity. Finally, he asked, "What do you think?"

"There was silence for a moment," he recalled. "Then Joan looked up at me with her beautiful blue eyes and said, 'But, Vic, haven't you, after all your studies, really come to believe Christ is the Son of God?'

"There was something about the way she said it and the way she looked at me that almost instantaneously knocked down all the barriers I had in my mind," he said. "All we had learned came together into a wonderful, magnificent, glowing, fabulous picture of Jesus.

"I hesitated, and then I said, 'Yes, I really do. I know it's true. I do believe!' I hadn't believed up until that point—but with the barriers torn down, I knew she was right. We moved into the living room and sat down on the couch. I said, 'So what about you?'

"She said, 'I settled the matter several days ago, but I was afraid to tell you. All the things we studied and learned finally convinced me about the Bible, about Christ, and about my need—*our* need—for him. A few days ago, I knew I was completely convinced.' She had already prayed to receive God's gift of forgiveness and eternal life. And that started the biggest adventure of our lives!"

Wanting to maximize the impact they would have, Viggo and Joan prayed a bold prayer in which they asked God to send them to a place where there were no Christians and no medical care. God obliged—and the Olsens ended up spending thirty-three years in the poverty-wracked nation of Bangladesh.

There they founded Memorial Christian Hospital as a center of medical care and spiritual light, where countless people have found healing and hope. They and their colleagues helped establish 120 churches. They were warmly embraced by the people and the government of Bangladesh. In fact, Viggo was honored with Visa #001 in gratitude for his contributions to the country.

"It must have been difficult to live in an underdeveloped nation like that," I said.

"Actually," he told me with a smile, "it was the greatest adventure we could ever have. When you're in a hard place, when you're over your head again and again, when you're sinking and beyond yourself and praying your heart out—then you see God reach out and touch your life and resolve the situation beyond anything you could have ever hoped."

His eyes sparkled. "There's nothing that can match that. We got to experience that again and again and again. We wouldn't have missed it for the world. In my opinion, finding the purpose for which God made you—whatever it may be—and then fully pursuing it is simply the very best way to live."

Viggo eventually wrote three books about his experiences. I especially like the title of one of them—*The Agnostic Who Dared to Search*—because it suggests there is a risk involved with investigating the evidence for God. At some point, the truth you uncover is going to demand a response.

And that could change everything.

## YOU WERE DESIGNED FOR DISCOVERY

Though Viggo Olsen has a stronger science background than I do, there were definite similarities in the way we both approached the issue of faith and science. We read books, we asked questions, we tracked down leads, and we pursued the evidence regardless of where it was taking us. We investigated systematically and enthusiastically, as if our lives depended on it.

And in the end, our lives, our attitudes, our philosophies, our worldviews, our priorities, and our relationships were revolutionized—for the better.

As I reviewed the avalanche of information from my investigation, I found the evidence for an Intelligent Designer to be believable and compelling. After combining that information with the historical evidence for Jesus being the unique Son of God, which I describe in my book *The Case for Christ*, putting my trust in the God of the Bible was nothing less than the most rational and natural decision I could make. I was merely permitting the torrent of facts to carry me along to their most logical conclusion.

If you're a spiritual skeptic or seeker, I hope you'll resolve to investigate the evidence for yourself. Actually, Olsen's three-pronged approach would provide a good outline to follow:

# Designed for Discovery

Astronomers are discovering a whole new dimension of evidence that suggests this astounding world was created, in part, so we could have the adventure of exploring it. As astronomer Guillermo Gonzalez and science philosopher Jay Wesley Richards, who wrote the book *The Privileged Planet*, told me in an interview:

- Total eclipses of the sun, which yield a treasure trove of scientific data, can only be viewed from one place in the solar system—and it "just happens" to be the only place in the solar system where there are intelligent beings to view them.
- Earth's location away from the galaxy's center and in the flat plane of the disk provides a particularly privileged vantage point for observing both nearby and distant stars.
- Earth provides an excellent position to detect the cosmic background radiation, which is critically important because it contains invaluable information about the properties of the universe when it was very young.
- Because our moon is the right size and distance to stabilize Earth's tilt, it helps preserve the deep snow deposits in our polar regions, from which scientists can determine the history of snowfall, temperatures, winds, and the amount of volcanic dust, methane, and carbon dioxide in the atmosphere.

The findings of scientists that our world appears to be designed for discovery have added a compelling new dimension to the evidence for a Creator. And, frankly, their analysis makes sense.

> If God so precisely and carefully and lovingly and amazingly constructed a mind-boggling habitat for his creatures, then it would be natural for him to want them to explore it, to measure it, to investigate it, to appreciate it, to be inspired by it—and ultimately, and most importantly, to find him through it. Wouldn't it?

- First, is there a God who created the universe?
- Second, did God reveal himself to humankind through the Bible or other sacred scriptures?
- Third, is Jesus the Son of God—deity united with humanity—who can help us as he claimed?

You'll soon find that the universe is governed by both physical laws and spiritual laws. The physical laws point us toward the Creator; the spiritual laws tell us how we can know him personally, both today and forever.

After all, he's not just the Creator in a broad sense; he's *your* Creator. You were made to relate to him in a vibrant, dynamic, and intimate way. And if you seek him wholeheartedly, he promises to provide all the clues you need to find him. In fact, you may even have sensed as you've been reading this book that he's already pursuing you in a subtle but very real way.

You were designed for discovery, as the latest research by astronomers suggests (see the box "Designed for Discovery"). And the greatest discovery of your life awaits you. So I hope you'll pursue scientific knowledge, but that you won't stop there. Don't let it become a destination; instead, allow it to guide you beyond itself to the incredible implications it offers for your life and eternity. In other words, let it point you to the Creator whom you can come to experience personally.

It will be the adventure of a lifetime.

# Notes

## Chapter 1

1. Linus Pauling, *No More War!* (New York: Dodd, Mead & Co., 1958), 209.

## Chapter 2

1. *Discover*, April 2002.
2. Steven Weinberg, *The First Three Minutes* (New York: Basic Books, updated ed., 1988), 5.
3. Weinberg, *First Three Minutes*, 6.
4. Brad Lemley, "Guth's Grand Guess," *Discover*, April 2002.
5. William Lane Craig and Quentin Smith, *Theism, Atheism and Big Bang Cosmology* (Oxford: Clarendon Press, 1993), 135.
6. Kai Nielsen, *Reason and Practice* (New York: Harper & Row, 1971), 48.
7. C. J. Isham, "Creation of the Universe as a Quantum Process," in R. J. Russell, W. R. Stoeger, and G. V. Coyne, eds., *Physics, Philosophy, and Theology* (Vatican City State: Vatican Observatory, 1988), 378, quoted in William Lane Craig, *Reasonable Faith* (Wheaton, Ill.: Crossway, rev. ed., 1994), 328.
8. Robert Jastrow, *God and the Astronomers*, rev. ed. (New York: W. W. Norton, 1992), 14.

## Chapter 3

1. These scientists published a full-page magazine advertisement under the banner "A Scientific Dissent from Darwinism." Their statement said: "We are skeptical of claims for the ability of random mutation and natural selection to account for the complexity of life." They added that "careful examination" of the evidence for Darwin's

theory "should be encouraged." See *The Weekly Standard* (October 1, 2001).

2. See Philip H. Abelson, "Chemical Events on the Primitive Earth," *Proceedings of the National Academy of Sciences USA* 55 (1966): 1365–72.

3. See Michael Florkin, "Ideas and Experiments in the Field of Prebiological Chemical Evolution," *Comprehensive Biochemistry* 29B (1975): 231–60.

4. See Sidney W. Fox and Klaus Dose, *Molecular Evolution and the Origin of Life*, rev. ed. (New York: Marcel Dekker, 1977), 43, 74–76.

5. John Cohen, "Novel Center Seeks to Add Spark to Origins of Life," *Science* 270 (1995): 1925–26.

6. See J. W. Valentine et al., "Fossils, Molecules, and Embryos: New Perspectives on the Cambrian Explosion," *Development* 126 (1999).

7. For a description of how various textbooks use embryo drawings, see Jonathan Wells, *Icons of Evolution* (Washington, D.C.: Regnery, 2000), 101–4.

8. Larry D. Martin, "The Relationship of *Archaeopteryx* to Other Birds," in M. K. Hecht, J. H. Ostrom, G. Viohl, and P. Wellnhofer, eds., *The Beginnings of Birds* (Eichstätt: Freunde des Jura-Museums, 1985), 182, quoted in Wells, *Icons of Evolution*, 116.

9. *World Book Encyclopedia* vol. 10 (Chicago: Field Enterprises Educational Corp., 1962 ed.), 50.

10. Marvin L. Lubenow, *Bones of Contention* (Grand Rapids: Baker, 1992), 87.

11. Hank Hanegraaff, *The Face That Demonstrates the Farce of Evolution* (Nashville: Word, 1998), 50.

12. See Philip E. Johnson, *Darwin on Trial*, 2nd ed. (Downers Grove, Ill.: InterVarsity Press, 1993), 126–27.

13. Douglas Futuyama, *Evolutionary Biology* (Sunderland, Mass.: Sinauer, 1986), 3.

14. See Lubenow, *Bones of Contention*, 86–99.

15. Hanegraaff, *Face*, 52.

16. Lubenow, *Bones of Contention*, 87.

17. Michael D. Lemonick, "How Man Began," *Time*, March 14, 1994, quoted in Hanegraaff, *Face*, 52.

18. See Constance Holden, "The Politics of Paleoanthropology," *Science* 213 (1981).

19. See Henry Gee, *In Search of Deep Time: Beyond the Fossil Record to a New History of Life* (New York: The Free Press, 1999).

## Chapter 4

1. Robin Collins, "A Scientific Argument for the Existence of God: The Fine-Tuning Design Argument," in Michael J. Murray, ed., *Reason for the Hope Within* (Grand Rapids: Eerdmans, 1999), 48.

2. Said Robin Collins: "The entire dial represents the range of force strengths in nature, with gravity being the weakest force and the strong nuclear force that binds protons and neutrons together in the nuclei being the strongest, a whopping ten thousand billion billion billion billion times stronger than gravity. The range of possible settings for the force of gravity can plausibly be taken to be at least as large as the total range of force strengths."

3. Walter L. Bradley, "The 'Just-So' Universe," in William A. Dembski and James M. Kushiner, eds., *Signs of Intelligence* (Grand Rapids: Brazos, 2001), 170.

4. Paul Davies, *God and the New Physics* (New York: Simon & Schuster, 1983), 189.

5. Edward Harrison, *Masks of the Universe* (New York: Collier Books, 1985), 252.

6. Fred Hoyle, "The Universe: Past and Present Reflections," *Annual Review of Astronomy and Astrophyicss* 20 (1982).

7. Paul Davies, *The Mind of God* (New York: Touchstone, 1992), 16, 232.

8. Owen Gingerich, "Dare a Scientist Believe in Design?" in John M. Templeton, ed., *Evidence of Purpose* (New York: Continuum, 1994), 25.

9. Stephen C. Meyer, "Evidence for Design in Physics and Biology," in Michael J. Behe, William A. Dembski, and Stephen C. Meyer,

*Science and Evidence for Design in the Universe* (San Francisco: Ignatius Press, 2000), 60.

10. See Brad Lemley, "Why Is There Life?" *Discover* (November 2002); and Martin Rees, *Just Six Numbers: The Deep Forces That Shape the Universe* (New York: Basic, 2000).

11. See Lemley, "Why Is There Life?"

12. Jimmy H. Davis and Harry L. Poe, *Designer Universe* (Nashville: Broadman & Holman, 2002), 107.

13. Robin Collins added that the one exception would be the rarely asserted view that these universes just exist on their own, without any cause, but many find this belief requires more faith than believing in a Creator!

14. Gregg Easterbrook, "The New Convergence," *Wired* (December 2002).

## Chapter 5

1. Charles Darwin, *The Origin of Species*, 6th ed. (New York: New York University Press, 1998), 154.

2. Bruce Alberts, "The Cell as a Collection of Protein Machines," *Cell* 92 (February 8, 1998).

3. Kenneth R. Miller, "The Flaw in the Mousetrap," *Natural History*, April 2002.

4. See Joe Lorio, "Four of a Kind," *Automobile*, August 2003.

5. Ibid., 147.

## Chapter 6

1. Quoted in Larry Witham, *By Design* (San Francisco: Encounter, 2003), 172.

2. See Nancy Gibbs, "The Secret of Life," *Time*, February 17, 2003.

3. Jim Brooks, *Origins of Life* (Sydney: Lion, 1985), np.

4. Michael Denton, *Evolution: A Theory in Crisis* (Chevy Chase, Md.: Adler & Adler, 1986), 261.

5. George Sim Johnson, "Did Darwin Get It Right?" *The Wall Street Journal*, October 15, 1999.

6. Francis A. Crick, *Life Itself* (New York: Simon & Schuster, 1981), 88.

## Chapter 7

1. Quoted in Candace Adams, "Leading Nanoscientist Builds Big Faith," *Baptist Standard*, March 15, 2002.
2. Stephen W. Hawking and Roger Penrose, *The Nature of Space and Time* (Princeton, N.J.: Princeton University Press, 1996), 20.
3. Psalm 102:25.
4. Nahum 1:3.
5. Psalm 104:24.
6. Psalm 33:5.

# About the Author

Lee Strobel, who holds a Master of Studies in Law degree from Yale Law School, as well as a journalism degree from the University of Missouri, is the former legal affairs editor of the *Chicago Tribune*. His awards include Illinois's highest honors for both investigative reporting (which he shared with a team he led) and public service journalism from United Press International.

He describes his journey from atheism to faith in the Gold Medallion–winning books *The Case for Christ* and *The Case for Faith*. His other bestsellers include *Inside the Mind of Unchurched Harry and Mary*, which also won a Gold Medallion; *Surviving a Spiritual Mismatch in Marriage*, which he coauthored with his wife, Leslie; *God's Outrageous Claims*; and *What Jesus Would Say*, all published by Zondervan. His book *Reckless Homicide* has been used as a supplementary text at several law schools.

Lee has been a teaching pastor at two of America's largest churches: Willow Creek Community Church in suburban Chicago and Saddleback Valley Community Church in Orange County, California. He is a contributing editor and columnist for *Outreach* magazine and formerly taught First Amendment Law at Roosevelt University.

Lee and Leslie, who have been married for more than thirty years, live in Southern California. Their daughter, Alison, is a teacher and novelist; their son, Kyle, received his master's degree in philosophy of religion and is pursuing a second master's degree in New Testament studies.

> *"My road to atheism was paved by science.... But, ironically, so was my later journey to God."*—Lee Strobel

# The Case for a Creator:
## *A Journalist Investigates Scientific Evidence That Points Toward God*

*Lee Strobel, Author of* The Case for Christ *and* The Case for Faith

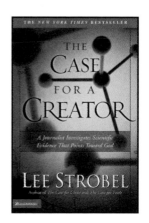

During his academic years, Lee Strobel became convinced that God was outmoded, a belief that colored his ensuing career as an award-winning journalist at the *Chicago Tribune*. Science had made the idea of a Creator irrelevant—or so Strobel thought.

But today science is pointing in a different direction. In recent years, a diverse and impressive body of research has increasingly supported the conclusion that the universe was intelligently designed. At the same time, Darwinism has faltered in the face of concrete facts and hard reason.

Has science discovered God? At the very least, it's giving faith an immense boost as new findings emerge about the incredible complexity of our universe. Join Strobel as he reexamines the theories that once led him away from God. Through his compelling and highly readable account, you'll encounter the mind-stretching discoveries from cosmology, cellular biology, DNA research, astronomy, physics, and human consciousness that present astonishing evidence in *The Case for a Creator*.

Hardcover: 0-310-24144-8
Unabridged Audio Pages® CD: 0-310-25439-6

ebooks:
Adobe Acrobat eBook Reader®: 0-310-25977-0
Microsoft Reader®: 0-310-25978-9
Palm™ Edition: 0-310-25979-7
Unabridged ebook Download: 0-310-26142-2

# The Case for Christ— Student Edition

*Lee Strobel with Jane Vogel*

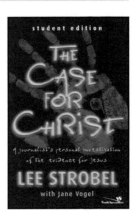

There's little question that he actually lived. But miracles? Rising from the dead? Some of the stories you hear about him sound like just that—stories. A reasonable person would never believe them, let alone the claim that he's the only way to God!

But a reasonable person would also make sure that he or she understood the facts before jumping to conclusions. That's why Lee Strobel—an award-winning legal journalist with a knack for asking tough questions—decided to investigate Jesus for himself. An atheist, Strobel felt certain his findings would bring Christianity's claims about Jesus tumbling down like a house of cards.

He was in for the surprise of his life. Join him as he retraces his journey from skepticism to faith. You'll consult expert testimony as you sift through the truths that history, science, psychiatry, literature, and religion reveal. Like Strobel, you'll be amazed at the evidence—how much there is, how strong it is, and what it says.

The facts are in. What will your verdict be in *The Case for Christ*?

Softcover 0-310-23484-0
Padded Hardcover Edition 0-310-24608-3

*Pick up a copy today at your favorite bookstore!*

**ZONDERVAN**™

GRAND RAPIDS, MICHIGAN 49530 USA

WWW.ZONDERVAN.COM

*A thought-provoking, fun-to-read student edition of*
The Case for Faith—*designed especially for teenagers.*

# The Case for Faith—
# Student Edition

*Lee Strobel with Jane Vogel*

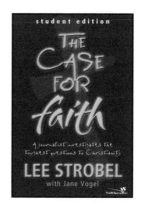

Despite the compelling historical evidence that Strobel presented in *The Case for Christ—Student Edition*, many people grapple with serious concerns about faith in God. As in a court of law, they want to shout, "Objection!" They say, "If there is a loving God, why is the world so full of suffering and evil?" Or, "If God really created the universe, why are so many scientists convinced that only evolutionary theory explains the origins of life?" Or, "If God really cares about the people he created, how could he consign so many of them to an eternity in hell?"

In *The Case for Faith—Student Edition*, Strobel turns his tenacious investigative skills to the most persistent emotional objections to belief—the eight "heart" barriers to faith. *The Case for Faith—Student Edition* is for those who may be feeling attracted to Jesus but who are faced with intellectual barriers standing squarely in their path. For Christians, it will deepen their convictions and give them fresh confidence in discussing Christianity with even their most skeptical friends.

Softcover 0-310-24188-X

*Pick up a copy today at your favorite bookstore!*

GRAND RAPIDS, MICHIGAN 49530 USA

WWW.ZONDERVAN.COM

# The Case for Christ

*A Journalist's Personal
Investigation of the
Evidence for Jesus*

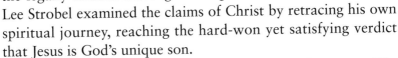

Is Jesus really the divine Son of God?
What reason is there to believe that he is?

In his bestseller *The Case for Christ*,
the legally trained investigative reporter
Lee Strobel examined the claims of Christ by retracing his own
spiritual journey, reaching the hard-won yet satisfying verdict
that Jesus is God's unique son.

Written in the style of a blockbuster investigative report, *The
Case for Christ* consults a dozen authorities on Jesus with doctorates from Cambridge, Princeton, Brandeis, and other top-
flight institutions to present:

- Historical evidence
- Psychiatric evidence
- Other evidence
- Scientific evidence
- Fingerprint evidence

This colorful, hard-hitting book is no novel. It's a riveting
quest for the truth about history's most compelling figure.

"Lee Strobel asks the questions a tough-minded skeptic
would ask. Every inquirer should have it."

—*Phillip E. Johnson, law professor,
University of California at Berkeley*

Hardcover 0-310-22646-5
Softcover 0-310-20930-7
Evangelism Pack 0-310-22605-8
Mass Market 6-pack 0-310-22627-9
Audio Pages® Abridged Cassette 0-310-24824-8
Audio Pages® Unabridged Cassette 0-310-21960-4
Audio Pages® Unabridged CD 0-310-24779-9

# The Case for Faith

*A Journalist Investigates the Toughest Objections to Christianity*

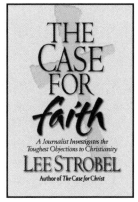

In his best-seller *The Case for Christ*, Lee Strobel examined the claims of Christ, reaching the hard-won yet satisfying verdict that Jesus is God's unique son.

But despite the compelling historical evidence that Strobel presented, many grapple with doubts or serious concerns about faith in God. As in a court of law, they want to shout, "Objection!" They say, "If God is love, then what about all of the suffering that festers in our world?" Or, "If Jesus is the door to heaven, then what about the millions who have never heard of him?"

In *The Case for Faith*, Strobel turns his tenacious investigative skills to the most persistent emotional objections to belief, the eight "heart" barriers to faith. *The Case for Faith* is for those who may be feeling attracted toward Jesus, but who are faced with formidable intellectual barriers standing squarely in their path. For Christians, it will deepen their convictions and give them fresh confidence in discussing Christianity with even their most skeptical friends.

Hardcover 0-310-22015-7
Softcover 0-310-23469-7
Evangelism Pack 0-310-23508-1
Mass Market 6-pack 0-310-23509X
Audio Pages® Abridged Cassettes 0-310-23475-1

*Pick up a copy today at your favorite bookstore!*

**ZONDERVAN**™

GRAND RAPIDS, MICHIGAN 49530 USA

WWW.ZONDERVAN.COM

# Inside the Mind of Unchurched Harry and Mary

*How to Reach Friends and Family Who Avoid God and the Church*

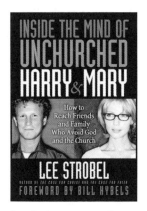

Who are unchurched Harry and Mary? He or she could be the neighbor who is perfectly happy without God. Or the co-worker who scoffs at Christianity. Or the supervisor who uses Jesus' name only as profanity. Or the family member who can't understand why religion is so important.

*Inside the Mind of Unchurched Harry and Mary* isn't a book of theory. It's an action plan to help Christians relate the message of Christ to the people they work around, live with, and call their friends. Using personal experiences, humor, compelling stories, biblical illustrations, and the latest research, Lee Strobel helps Christians understand unbelievers and what motivates them.

The book includes:

- 15 key insights into why people steer clear of God and the church
- A look at Christianity and its message through the eyes of a former atheist
- Practical, inspirational strategies for building relationships with unbelievers
- Firsthand advice on surviving marriage to an unbelieving spouse.

Softcover 0-310-37561-4

*Pick up a copy today at your favorite bookstore!*

**ZONDERVAN**™

GRAND RAPIDS, MICHIGAN 49530 USA

WWW.ZONDERVAN.COM

# What Jesus Would Say

*To: Rush Limbaugh, Madonna, Bill Clinton, Michael Jordan, Bart Simpson, Donald Trump, Murphy Brown, Madalyn Murphy O'Hair, Mother Teresa, David Letterman, & You!*

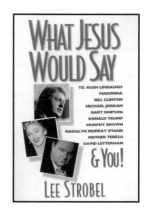

In *What Jesus Would Say*, Lee Strobel helps us to see well-known personalities as Jesus might see them. Through these people, Strobel introduces us to the God of hope, the God of the second chance.

*What Jesus Would Say* takes on topics such as success, sexuality, skepticism, forgiveness, prayer, and leadership with firm, biblically based concepts. In his often surprising look into the lives of famous people, Strobel shares encouraging and inspiring ideas that apply to our own lives as well.

What would Jesus say to today's headline-makers . . . and to you?

Softcover 0-310-48511-8

*Pick up a copy today at your favorite bookstore!*

**ZONDERVAN**™

GRAND RAPIDS, MICHIGAN 49530 USA

WWW.ZONDERVAN.COM

We want to hear from you. Please send your comments about this book to us in care of zreview@zondervan.com. Thank you.

GRAND RAPIDS, MICHIGAN 49530 USA

WWW.ZONDERVAN.COM